THE GUNFIGHTER'S GUIDE TO BUSINESS

THE GUNFIGHTER'S GUIDE TO BUSINESS

A Skelton Key to Western Civilization's Mastery of the future

By
Rich Hoffman

LIBERTY HILL PUBLISHING

Liberty Hill Publishing
2301 Lucien Way #415
Maitland, FL 32751
407.339.4217
www.libertyhillpublishing.com

Cover designed by: Holly Denham
Photography by: Brooke Townsend

Paperback ISBN-13: 978-1-6628-2320-6
Ebook ISBN-13: 978-1-6628-2321-3

CONTENTS

INTRODUCTION

When I first started this book, the intention was to help business people have a strategy guide for their day-to-day lives in a corporate setting. Still, as it became more apparent throughout the research and study of the contents, it essentially evolved into a general strategy for global politics. After the extraordinary events of 2020, politically, it was clear how much corporations influence our day-to-day life. Whether or not we do work for them, nor passively interact with them at the level of politics, or as a global health crisis and our social reaction to it, the clarity of these events were essentially macrocosms of the microcosm of a business climate and the idea of Constitutional Natural Law. Today's businessperson has to deal with the internal struggles of their industry and the politics of the global marketplace and the negative or positive philosophies that conduct the behavior. For success to be born in the sometimes very hostile environment of modern social challenges is a strategy for pulling it all together and not only surviving but thriving. To not be a victim of circumstance, but a perpetrator of success, success measured in every way that it can be estimated, with dollars and cents, as well as personal and social respect.

Without getting into the specifics of Natural Law, it is the most apparent debilitating cause of much of the world's troubles when its relationship is lost. History from the American Revolution to the start of the Progressive Era saw many conflicts and spilled blood, a lot of it. It was upon these forces which gave rise to the freedom of slaves, the establishment of equal rights among the sexes, and the most rapid expansion of a country known to the world. With those types of issues being born and coming into conflict with the powers of tradition, violence, and the gun's birth as we know it today was no surprise. Moving from an obscure spot on the globe with no real economy to become the world's superpower giving the skyline of New York a spectacle, unlike the world had ever seen before, made this period a miracle to the eyes of humankind. The wealth built during this time and how businesses evolved truly did evolve with each shootout that Wild Bill Hickock blasted from his dual pistols. Hickock was a natural gunfighting progression of icons like Daniel Boone, Kit Carson, and many other frontier sharpshooters. There would be others who would take those legends of bravery and honor and carry Natural Law into the assumption that the Wild West would evolve into a place of opportunity mixed with morality as blazing six-shooters paved the way with a new kind of philosophy. This one not from the Orient or the Greek ruins.

Rather than looking at the world as it is now, a place that has lost contact with Natural Law after that period of 1890 onward, to get to the magic of how to win and prosper from a western civilization perspective, an honest embrace of this Wild West period should not only be explored but embraced so that we can return to that same ambition and honor as we move into space to start new frontiers of adventure, prosperity, and excitement. We must not only understand how wayward adventurers discovered the magic for the first time in the history of the world but to duplicate it again, pointing our guns back to business and using those guns to rediscover Natural Law as it has always been at our fingertips.

To assume that modern business has no relationship with such an old idea of Natural Law is to forget everything we treasure as a society and our hopes to create wealth for our families, business professionals, and countries. Purposely we do not explore Natural Law in the rest of this book because, as a reader, it deprives the experience of rediscovering it through the revelations of the contents. It is essential to know that when gunslingers went to work in defense of justice, they understood right and wrong naturally for proper context in the realm of good and evil as it exists in the universe. An 1870s gunslinger wouldn't have been thinking about the justice of the planet Jupiter using its massive gravitational pull to save the earth from constant asteroid bombardment enabling life to evolve in cosmic peace for 30,000 years. Just enough time to allow humanity to escape to space before extinction arrives like a bandit to rob us of our hopes. Or the white blood cell that works in our bodies to fight off a new disease or shake off the false masks of a cancer cell to hide dormant in a healthy body until they are ready to make their move to kill the host. We could say the same about political attackers in our governments or our businesses. There are always rivals wanting to kill us off over internal jealousies that desire to rip down the good and promote the bad in an ever quest for power and control fulfilled with an illustrious nameplate above the door.

With Wyatt Earp and Doc Holliday shooting it out with villains in the streets of Dodge City, we saw a yearning for justice by average people equipped with their guns to fight for a better world. Then Seth Bullock of Deadwood was slinging guns with the legendary Wild Bill for the exact cause. Among the worst of the crime, the prostitutes and the Hell on Earth living conditions in a lawless society, there was a yearning for Natural Law, for good guys to stand for something even if they tried but fell short. In the attempt to emulate the laws of the universe and stand for good, for growth, for something as the forces of decline were ever-present, we saw in the gunfighters a need for justice as gunsmoke danced through history shaking everything into an eventual collapse.

A gunfighter has more in common with the ambitions of business than the carefully groomed appendage of academia. Often those academic forces are shaped by the forces of chaos to mask the inadequacies of the come lately types, the Dandies. The Dandies loot off the bravery and ambitions of the gunfighters as they stand down and face danger in whatever circumstance it presents itself, either as another villain on a dusty street or a business tycoon trying to stay alive through government regulations and hostile political parties. It's all the same game and one of the most understudied topics in the world.

I would offer that what you have here is a kind of skeleton key to the success of western civilization and a defense of the business practices which evolved out of a desire for Natural Law contemplated by the American Constitution. These desires played out in the dusty streets of boomtowns before the 20th Century. The Bounty Hunters and the Dandies' role was to loot off the backs of the ambitious, bold, and legends that don't always notice as civilization often erases their memory under the banners of chaos and industry. We know of Wild Bill and Wyatt Earp because the media fell in love with them and told stories of their adventures taming the Wild West as commerce moved and thrived about growing into the skyscrapers we see today. But little is known about Bass Reeves, the frontier lawman who happened to be black and was the inspiration for The Lone Ranger. But that doesn't mean that such people aren't necessary in the building of law, order, and commerce, for which our topic here desperately yearns. And for which we begin to tell a story that needs to be said and is as relevant if not more so than it was in previous centuries.

Rich Hoffman 2021

Roswell, New Mexico February 15th

EAST MEETS WEST

In business, there seems to be a general acceptance that the operations of the East are superior to those of the West and that all education and reverence should look no further into the matter, accepting that assessment at face value. That is pretty much where most of today's bounty hunters function, which I disagree with vehemently. I don't think any truth is more twisted than in this basic assumption of East meeting West. When American businesspeople go to trade shows or shake hands with others worldwide, there is a lot of silent brimming that goes on once all the inhabitants of a meeting have cleared the room. After all, members of Western business are considered reckless cowboys who are too impatient and often shoot from the hip too often and too quickly. There is a reputation in the East for precision and patience that makes them seem far superior, and to my experience, this is not the case at all.

The many battles between Eastern and West cultures have always been an argument over nature versus creative imagination. In the Greeks, Romans, and eventually, the Renaissance art of Europe essentially formed the foundations of Western culture and the eventual cowboy sentiments. In the East, the Egyptians migrated into the Indus Valley, and eventually, China taking with them the rigidity of the city-state. The discipline of the East was impressive; it still is today, whereas in the West, cultures have ebbed and flowed in and out of existence, and many, many wars fought. The East had its conflicts also, mainly when it came to the Mongols invasion of Genghis Khan into China which effectively ran the world of global politics during his time. Eventually, the exploits of Khan faded into the empire of the Ming Dynasty early in the 15th Century, and it was the great fleet commander Zheng He who likely brought the American Indian to the New World.

Even more likely going back to the Egyptians, fleet trade across the Atlantic and Pacific were going on by Asian cultures. They were quite aware of the New World and frequently made trips and established colonies to supply flourishing markets. By the time the Europeans were able to build their own ships to cross the great oceans, they chose not to acknowledge the history of the Orient as part of the recognized maritime achievement. In Europe, it was the conquering Vikings who had moved to the New World with their advanced ships at a time before Khan's empire did the same. As the Vikings conquered the known world in their day, spectacularly destroying many cultures leftover from the age of Rome's push into northern Europe and filling that power vacuum, they too made their way into North America. By the time Christopher Columbus found the maps of the world already charted showing it was round, that North and South America were out there to the West if only they could get there, which of course they did, it was Europe that was last to the New World across the Atlantic. Over the next 200 years, cultures of the West flowed further in that direction where they met cultures of the East already there from centuries prior.

The East did have what the West didn't, was continuity under the various empires to invent. Their cultures may have never experienced much personal freedom, such as Europe did under the Roman Empire or the Renaissance. Still, they did learn how to work together to satisfy their emperors. Under those conditions, gunpowder was invented by accident, conducting experiments pursuing the elixir of life under the vast umbrella of experimental medicine that had become known in the East during the 9th Century. While the East invented gunpowder, the West learned to use it to the most significant effect. For the Orient bound to nature and the oppressive force of emperors and rulers over the many years of their history, they struggled with new inventions. As directly established by the Egyptians, the Orient struggled to advance as a culture that came well before them. It was the rebellious West who used gunpowder to revolt against tyranny and led wars for personal freedom. This new philosophy of gunpowder connected to political persuasion eventually culminated in the pirate movement in the Caribbean during the 17th Century. It unleashed the Revolutionary

War a mere hundred years later. Learning to make guns for the invented gunpowder and use them on the battlefield once East met West in the war-like confrontation wasn't in Europe as many might have thought due to the politics of the Silk Road. What came out of North America was a mystery to early Silk Road trading, which allowed for cultures to avoid their differences in commerce. Europe itself wasn't ready to deal with the nature of personal independence as the wars were fought by factions of their thinking, first in the various revolutions, then in North America itself between the North and the South within these borders of New Worlds.

As Christopher Columbus called them Indians, the people who migrated East from the Orient weren't much of a match for the people of the West with their guns and inventions of industry. The nature-loving Orientals clashed in North America with the never-happy greed of personal growth and opportunity that came out of Europe, and it was never a contest. While the conflict could have easily define where the Orient met Europe, the real fight wouldn't occur until those forces met in North America, where the Indians were wholly pushed back into the Pacific. While the morality of this portion of history varies based on the point of view, the results are apparent. Without gunpowder and guns, the quest for individual freedom never would have occurred. This force essentially ran down the Oriental-based Indians when the Western-based cowboys and gunfighters met them on the plains of the Wild West.

The industry that came after was born from the freedom of free people functioning out of self-interest, and the economy of Western culture erupted. Many methods of business that emerged out of that creation have been unexplored. The past resentments are still very much part of our daily discussions, even if many have forgotten why. However, shooting from the hip and the reckless antics of the West are assets, not detriments. It's time to defend what worked so well in the West, perhaps for the first time. While it is easy to admire the precision and patience of eastern cultures, the West overcame those methods with sheer force and determination. Simultaneously, the Indians used bows and arrows, not much different from when Genghis Khan used them from horseback to establish an empire. In the West, guns were developed out of a need for Manifest Destiny to overcome the tyranny of groupthink over individual ambition. That became the very definition of success in the West. And that same trait is why it was in the West, not the East, that the most significant economies sprung forth. It wasn't by accident or even superior ideas. For the first time, individuals armed with guns kept tyranny from ruling over their minds which brought to blossom invention and the businesses that matured from that effort—a new way of thinking born a unique opportunity for achievement that had never yet experienced attention in the arts of philosophy.

CHAPTER NOTES:

a. The assumption that the East is superior to the West is incorrect. It all comes down to philosophy, and shooting from the hip in Western cultures does not mean recklessness. It's all about speed and accuracy.
b. The two philosophies of the East and the West spent many thousands of years avoiding each other until the cultures collided during the cowboys meeting the Indians in North America.
c. It came down to the invention of gunpowder and how the philosophies developed it into economic activity and personal governance.
d. The new economy of personal fulfillment was different from those functioning under centralized government and unleashed an explosion of growth worldwide.

CHISUM

The Lincoln County War, for my record, is one of the most evident and impressive sagas in American history. In the context of the world, an actual testimony to the success and failures of the human race. It features a person I greatly respect, John Chisum, played by John Wayne in the popular 1970s movie. However, Chisum was even more significant than life for what Wayne could portray on screen in this case. As a highly wealthy cattle baron who made his fortune taming half of New Mexico when nobody else had the guts, John Chisum provided the context for much of what this book professes. Before formal government and country namesake, wealth creation and business management had a chance to take deep root in the public consciousness. In the center of New Mexico was one of the largest counties in the young United States, Lincoln County, and the town named after it where the heart and soul of business commerce and its merits emerged through much turmoil. It all started with John Chisum's grand ambitions turned to wealth and finished many murders and gunfights later established the heart of justice as gun smoke drifted across the New Mexican desert. A villain of great report, Lawrence Murphy, typical of industry titans of later years, built a store in the middle of Lincoln and wanted to maintain a monopoly there until Chisum and his partner John Tunstall decided to bring justice with a store of their own.

Lawrence Murphy and his partner James Dolan had in mind to erode Chisum's great cattle empire by manipulating the law against the baron, which was the cause of the great war there in Lincoln County. Chisum had come to New Mexico with all litigiousness removed from society at the time. Where hard work and determination could pave the way to fame and fortune, those like Murphy, who didn't have such courage, of course, did as all villains do, sought to steal that wealth away as Chisum had made it. Murphy had the legal system of New Mexico in his pocket up to the governor of the state, Lew Wallace—the eventual author of *Ben Hur*. However, in the town of Lincoln, Murphy had complete control over the sheriff, William Brady, who helped orchestrate the murder of Chisum's business partner John Tunstall. And as it so happened, Tunstall had been a friend and mentor to the young Billy the Kid. Upon the murder of Tunstall, Billy the Kid killed Sheriff Brady, and the gloves were then off for much bloodshed and mayhem.

Thinking like a gunfighter, it was ultimately by the hands of the gun and the murderous antics of Kid and his gang of outrageous outlaws who brought justice to Lincoln County and New Mexico in general and opened it to the needs of all who followed. Billy the Kid had to kill off Brady as a member of the law. In the context of the war, the law was used politically for crushing the good, robbing Chisum of all the excellent work and business he had built over his lifetime. Yet in business, there are always Murphy types and villains like James Dolan who can speak politely to your face. At the same time, they build alliances against the good to rob them of their worth, and sometimes it takes a Billy the Kid to come along and root out justice where it's not so obvious. Brady was the representative of the law, the lawbreakers, the villains. Within processes such as this, much evil emerges in the world. It took an outlaw gunfighter and a cattle baron to bring value and justice out in the open.

Every businessperson must come to terms with themselves relative to some character in the Lincoln County War. Every character in the drama could represent every type of personality witnessed in modern corporate culture. Yet history knows who ultimately wins in these encounters, and by some miracle, the villains never end up coming out on top. In this story, by the time Tunstall felt the sting of an assassin's bullet by Murphey's gunfighters in February of 1878, the villain himself was dead by October of that same year, taking with him the manipulations and arrogance of his thievery, which is always the case with these types of insurgents. They are too lazy to make it in the world for themselves and are always looking to loot from others, which not so oddly enough carries over into their general health. Ultimately, such people are too lazy to live when denied the efforts of exemplary businesspeople like John Chisum. Murphy died at the age of 47, and the Lincoln County War sputtered to an end, but not before more lives were victims of slapped leather in blazes of attempted glory and ambitious gain. By then, all eyes turned to Billy the Kid, who was hiding out in the modern-day Ruidoso region, which to this very time can be a scene of aspiration and hope in the world should one ever want to take a vacation. The noted hideouts of the outlaw gunfighter Billy the Kid are everywhere. Nobody remembers Lawrence Murphy, but everyone knows over 100 years later Billy the Kid. And right in downtown Roswell New Mexico is the great statue of John Chisum, who had first brought value to that remote desert and, in his wake, civilization and freedom.

Like all businesspeople, Chisum saw an opportunity and utilized it to all his efforts building great wealth and opportunity for all who came after him, even to this very day. Many will only think of Roswell as the place where a flying saucer might have crashed, and the government came in and attempted to cover it all up. But well before any of that happened, or the nuclear tests of World War II, there was John Chisum, Billy the Kid, John Tunstall, and many others who threw ambition and courage to the wind to carve out of nothing the value of something new. Since the time of John Chisum, every entrepreneur and businessperson could tell a similar story literally or figuratively. What was unique about Chisum was that he showed what one person could do who was not held down by government rules and regulations or money barriers. Before he came along, not many people saw what could occur out of such a lonely place like New Mexico. But once Chisum showed the value, many villains came in his wake in the form of gunfighters and legal thieves to steal what they could while they could manage to stay alive. Of course, many desperate villains could tell ghost stories like these in every corporation of the modern era. Some might say that it would have been better had Chisum, or any business for that matter, never had the opportunity, that many more people would be alive in such a violent world. Yet thinking like a gunfighter, such business enterprises are worth it because of the good left in their wake, so meeting the trouble in its face is why the courage of such times is worth studying in the present.

CHAPTER NOTES:

a. John Chisum was a great cattle baron who settled in New Mexico and owned half of the state leading to the well-known Lincoln County War.
b. Lawrence Murphy was a political business rival working against Chisum who used the rules of a litigious society to attack the great cattle empire.
c. Murphy used a sheriff loyal to him to orchestrate the murder of Chisum's business partner John Tunstall which then set Billy the Kid on a murderous rampage.
d. All business people could find a version of themselves in the Lincoln County War. The lesson is that society's villainous law and order mechanisms can steal from the good and virtuous, such as the wealthy job creators like John Chisum.

THE AGE OF GUNFIGHTERS

These days, the Old West period is shown in parody, with a hefty dose of comedy, especially in live shows. I know many live Western acts use some version of comic stereotypes when representing the period because that is how we have come to remember it. So the question needs to be answered, why pick this period for an examination into business foundations? That answer comes into focus when the tract of history that we are all on comes into consideration, which for me occurred during a business trip to Japan that happened not too long before a similar trip to London and Paris. I couldn't help but notice that cowboy Westerns were how they stereotyped us, and I didn't find that a bad thing. In Japan, they have a leftover samurai culture active during this period of historical development, which is still very much alive in their modern culture. Giving the topic thought came to my mind that shying away from our past in America needed to stop. The Western culture we all lived into some degree or another needed to be honored more than rejected as parody.

For many very complicated reasons, the Old West period in North America was a special one with very historical significance. I'll be one of the last people in the world to say we want to go back to that time, a period of 1865 to about 1890. I like air conditioning, running water and modern food. I also like science and the prospect of new inventions, and in that regard, space certainly is the new frontier. I'm not suggesting that we all go back to Wild West towns only to waste our days playing poker and drinking our lives away as some of the most personally destructive gunfighters did during the period of the American West. However, that referenced period did have a meaning that occurred for the first time in human history. It directly involved the invention of the gun and how people used them to usher in a new age and economic theory.

Many of the books on business that are most studied today focus on practices that have occurred since the two World Wars. For many, the world of business management starts there and ends somewhere in the many versions of the bounty hunters attempt to blend Eastern approaches to Western mindsets. Yet business had been occurring in the human mind for many thousands of years. The street vendor in Phoenicia had a lot more in common with the modern kiosk operator in a local shopping mall than many might consider, but it's very accurate. Business and its conduct have been going on for a very long time. Very little has changed over that duration, essentially until America happened from the 1750s to the indicated time of 1890. During that magical yet very bloody period, humankind decided to clash with the rest of the world. Still, meanings of existence were redefined forever and should express thanks to the legends of the gunfighters.

The five big wars that occurred over this indicated period were the French and Indian War, the American Revolution, The War of 1812, The Texas Revolution, and the Civil War. Much hard blood flowed with much misery and hardship during this period, and the one of Western Expansion that followed, giving rise to the gunslingers and outlaws of what we call the Old West today. Of course, during this entire time, businesses thrived, and people made money building great family names along the way. But what was different in these periods of wars was that humanity decided it would self-rule and defend private assets for the first time in the history of the known world. Wars weren't going to erupt over the honor of kings, queens, and emperors, but over individual rights, such as was the case of the Civil War. From that culture, the idea of the American gunfighter became a reality that existed nowhere else at any other point in history, and it changed the way America interacted with everyone else.

The old gunslinger mindset emerged in businessmen like Henry Ford, and Howard Hughes contributed to innovation. Still, for the most part, the 20th Century desired to move into a more global society, whereas in America, that went against the nature of those wars mentioned dramatically, leaving the typical resident of North America feeling torn in two. The lessons learned from the American period of Western Expansion were criticized unfairly and eventually lost to our modern generations. But the gunslinger is still very much alive in all of us. We love them when we see them, whether it's in sports or business, and secretly we revere that time when such people lived with a lot of hope that we won't lose those traits as a nation. Which given my point of view, allowing such a thing to happen would genuinely be a tragedy. America started an excellent foundation for a new way of looking at many things, particularly in business. But what we built on it since that time isn't necessarily good, and perhaps it's time to revisit those values and defend their birth.

That is why an emphasis on the gunfighter exploded during the short time after Civil War when Reconstruction pushed people and their beliefs to their limits and would shape our future forever. A new kind of human being evolved onto the stage self-determined and hungry to make a life for themselves, not for some noble territorial overlord. That is undoubtedly the motivation of the average American worker to this very day. We don't work for institutions and systems of control; we do it for our preservation and gain. Learning to manage such people for a productive enterprise takes a unique look at the matter. Nothing touches all our minds more than the world of business because most of us all work somewhere and in many ways have direct input into the kind of culture those places are. And to do that, we must know what kind of people we are and why we became that way. To that understanding, most love the American gunfighters even pushed back in our imaginations and satirized to the point of lunacy. Yet, they are what make us different and are at the foundations of our national character. Without the gunfighter, I don't think we would have had Elon Musk or Steve Jobs. I think Thomas Edison would have remained a deaf eccentric playing with electronics uneventfully at his mom's home. I don't think we would have seen great companies like General Electric come off those Edison efforts or even Hollywood's market emerge. We are what we are because of the great gunslingers who tamed the frontier allowing for the first time in history; the western thinking of Aristotle and many others proved that humans could rule themselves. The key to significant economies and national power came not from kings but from the gun-carrying individuals who just wanted their slice of the pie.

Learning to manage such people toward a business enterprise, we must understand the nature of such a period that emerged and remember how we all got there.

CHAPTER NOTES:

a. The Old West period is a great way to step back and analyze what we have learned in America through history and honor what built our nation, and stand behind the successes which emerged.
b. Many books on businesses miss what Western Civilization brings to the unique and invented world for the first time in human history.
c. Gunfighters were a different kind of warrior in the world. What came in their wake was economic expansion unlike anything ever known, the acknowledgment of individual rights instead of defending feudal lords and houses of royalty.
d. The key to management is to align business needs with employee self-interest and not a reliance on institutional sacrifice.

CHARGING HELL WITH A BUCKET OF WATER

One of the most significant needs in the business community is why looking at the world as a gunfighter is essential instead of all the other methods currently in the marketplace. The wrong philosophies manage businesses and their affairs too often because there is a failure to recognize good people and bad people globally, making it impossible to deal fairly in all interactions. Suppose you try to mitigate bad people from harming good people. In that case, often, management methods are watered down in effectiveness because of the failure to identify the real cause of a company's trouble. When good people find themselves ignored for their good deeds, they will either give up trying to apply it to the work culture or leave for some other destination, making employee acquisition difficult. Ineffective companies trying to throw money at their inability to define good and evil in their workplace end up driving out the good and attracting evil. The reason is that good people don't just work for money, but their total value of experience.

We all have seen the signs. Many reading this book are active participants in this behavior, so everyone knows the unsaid rules. People do not naturally get along. If they don't share values, they won't work well together. The task of management is often to use various consultant methods developed over the years so that good people and bad people can work together toward a common objective, which can lead to some limited success. However, if bad people are present, there will always be a pull to retreat into the abyss of negativity that permeates most companies and their work cultures. Vile, evil people will often say one thing to their peers' faces, but they talk wrong about them when they have left the room. They use many passive-aggressive tactics to attempt to rip down their corporate enemies in sometimes very despicable ways, all so that they can gain a little power under the company that employs them.

The truth of the matter was firearms were invented because there are good guys and bad guys worldwide, and they come in all forms of sexes and races. To the best of our knowledge of God and the afterlife, that's the way creation was conceived. As humans, it has been left to us to pick a side and advance or decline our civilization based on these rules of the great game, which is fully observable in nature. Companies are no less the battleground of our modern times where good and evil play out in sometimes very scandalous ways. It helps nobody to pretend that these factors are not part of any corporate structure; it's naive to think otherwise. That certainly doesn't mean that you take up the flag of goodness and run around gunning down all the villains in your life. However, it does mean we should take what we have learned from the early days of capitalism to understand the mind of the gunfighter and how that could apply to bringing justice to any workplace. Not with violence, but with the tactics and understanding that helped gunfighters live and die during the creation of America and its vast economy.

Most people are good and evil in their lives, depending on where they are along their aging process. In that regard, villains and heroes are constantly swapping hats so that a good guy today might have been a bad guy yesterday over the life of employment at a company. A gunfighter's mind would understand that all people tend both, and they would plan accordingly. It is unwise to assume that any act of good or an effort at productivity would garner respect from your peers. Instead, the reality is quite the opposite. Co-workers will often despise the company do-gooder or the puritan who wants to do good company work for their employers because it raises the standard for everyone else. Bad people don't want their standards raised; they want to consistently lower them. It wouldn't be a complicated science experiment to identify that laziness and evil go hand in hand. Many people will do bad things so that they don't have to work too hard. That is why they become bad so that they can live off the efforts of others and take what doesn't belong to them. So long as imperfect people live in the world, the good, hard-working, honest people of the world will constantly be attacked, slandered, and find conspiracy aimed at them. The higher up the ladder of success you find yourself, the worse it gets. Many at the top of the corporate world find they have to become bad guys because they spend so much time fighting off the inadequate efforts of others that they become what they think about most and find themselves converted over to evil. That is not the path to a good company or proper management.

Thinking like a gunfighter, knowing how to defend yourself with the ease of having the ultimate equalizer on your holstered hip is the best way to mitigate evil actions against you. Just as carrying a gun with a CCW will help relax the anxiety that can come about from threats of robbery, assault, or just random terrorism, taking that same mentality into the corporate world will peel away quickly the attempts of evil to denounce the good. No consultants can help a company thrive if they don't deal with this inherent problem of good people and bad people being thrown together in a workplace. When the bad will do just about anything to hold down the excellent, nobody can raise the expectations of all to something very beneficial to whatever company is attempting such a thing. In companies and life in general, bad people need eradicating. In the days of the first gunfighters, they would be filled with lead by the gunslingers. These days we must be much more subtle about our methods, but the results are the same. It is the good that makes a company good or bad.

You won't have a bad company filled with good people—the good people will leave as the scum stays behind. It is up to those who manage those companies to distinguish good from bad people and make the good honorable and rewarded while ostracizing the bad. If the bad is left to terrorize the good and convert them into bad employees, they will follow into a bad condition. If these elements are not recognized, then failure will follow, and everyone in the process will fail and become the victim of evil people's antics. One of the problems of our age is that we have been unable to identify good and bad people in our society, leaving many elements of our civilization falling to evil. And when such times existed on the open plains of Western Expansion where the law was far and few between, the only justice that was possible came from gunfighters and the personal ownership of guns to protect the good from the bad.

CHAPTER NOTES:

a. To manage appropriately in a business environment, it is essential to identify good people and empower them to overcome bad people.
b. Firearms were invented in the world to protect good behavior from the intentions of bad behavior.
c. Most people have the potential for good and evil. It is up to creating a good work culture to understand how to evoke the good traits and avoid the bad.
d. Bad people hate good people because they are lazy and want to keep the expectations low and easy for them to fulfill.

THE TRIGGERNOMETRY OF POKER

Most of us will not be managing our own large multi-billion-dollar companies and are not on the get-rich-quick path to personal wealth. Most businesspeople in America will be playing with house money, meaning they are managing on behalf of an owner or a board of directors of some kind. Those are the people counting on businesspeople they hire to do them well at the excellent business game. That is why I have always viewed the role of business management by the superb card game of poker, specifically. In poker, the game is about playing the hands you get from the deck and deciding how much value you can extract from them without losing too much on the mandatory bets each round.

Poker is this game when you are playing with a lot of people at the table. In business, if you are trying to win a large job contract or manage a mature account with many players in it, you want to play aggressively but bet as little as possible before the flop to see how everyone reacts to the conditions of the game. Before the bets get too high, depending on the first three cards on the table show and how they match up to the cards you have been dealt, you want to push up the pot to see if you can knock out some of the other players. Once some dropout, you can improve your odds of winning once the river card arrives upon the table. If you manage to play with only one or two other people remaining and have some high card pairs, you can play to kill. If not, you can fold and get out of the round without throwing away a lot of money. In business, this is how you have to look at the conditional elements at play. The natural risk-takers, the owners, and boards of directors depend on their businesspeople to mitigate their chances at the table by understanding these subtle rules. How the game is played decides how well their endeavor goes.

The gunfighter, of course, is often hired to manage games of poker; traditionally, saloons hired them to stand over the increased pots that gathered to make sure everyone played fair. Otherwise, they'd be shot and killed. It wasn't uncommon for the best gunfighters to become major poker players themselves; Wild Bill Hickock comes to mind. Guns and poker go together, especially in the classic sense of being a gunfighter. The risk and rewards associated with these games can be very alluring, so it's not uncommon for such a power to go to the players' heads. They end up with severe drinking habits or problems with promiscuity. Those who win most and do the best for their companies keep their heads cool, mitigate their risks, and out leverage their opponents.

It is alright to play with low cards in the early levels of a poker game that might add up to a flush so long as there aren't high bets at the table. However, when the pot increases and most people at the table fold, leaving you still in the game, nobody should settle for anything less than the highest percentage of matchups. If you don't have the cards, then fold and keep your chips on an upward trajectory. Players who think that they have to keep pushing all their chips are bound to be losers because the odds are against them from the start. They may win a few 50/50 matchups, but by default, they won't win them all. Luck isn't as much about playing poker as it is skill and patience. If the cards aren't there, don't play them.

And that is the same as in gunfighting. You are pulling a fast draw against another player to hit a target under .500 of a second at a distance of 15 feet or more means that the shooter must draw and aim insanely fast. The temptation is to draw and get the gun out in front of you to improve your aim. But in the process, precious time is lost in the speed. What is best is to shoot the gun coming out of the holster; the bullet travels much faster than the hand holding the gun. I tend to think of this shooting as playing the river in poker where only one or two players are left playing the round. You must trust your skills. You may draw, shoot and miss. At such a speed, it is easy to miss. If you are good and have worked hard to have the skills to win, then you must trust yourself just as you must trust your cards. If you start pushing up the bets and doing things you wouldn't normally do, then your chances of missing increase dramatically. Gunfighting and poker are very much of the same mind, making them essential contributors to success or failure. If you are not using the game rules to your advantage, the rules will be used against you. There is no in-between thought process.

Bluffing is very much a part of the game of poker, just as it is in gunfighting. In both cases, when you are at the line and the pressure is on, you have to trust your training, roll with your instincts built from experience, and let the cards fall where they may, mitigating your risks as much as possible. That is, after all, why businesspeople are hired to manage the game. Business owners have taken a lot of risks just to put all the cards in play. It's too much to ask most of them to make sure the game stays fair, and that money is generated from the process of playing. That is how we say in America, "we make money." Money doesn't just exist by itself. We produce as a capitalist culture the value of our products. The poker table is just a thing until the game brings value to it. By the rules of the game, the participants play their cards and place value into the pot—a competition to capture those gains in business is the sole objective. Nothing else matters. Playing the game means that all the skills of acquiring that wealth will be needed, including bluffing to control the actions of your opponents. Those who are good at holding firm under pressure are better at it than those who fear anxiety. That is the reason so many gunfighters traditionally did very well at poker.

Think of standing in a line against a duel with another human being, knowing that at the draw of a gun, everything you ever were and might ever become could be eliminated by a rival in an instant. Those who did it straight and not trying to kill an opponent in the back while they were drunk had to hold firm to perform the task. The risks and rewards were quite clear. So conquering those fears, gunfighters were at a severe advantage when playing poker against others who had not yet conquered those fears. That is why thinking in the way of a gunfighter can make great businesspeople. It puts their minds more at ease with the risks associated with the game. What is certain is that it's not possible to win every round because you are not in control of what cards you are dealt. But what you do control is how you play those cards. Sometimes with bluffing, sometimes with just patience, sometimes with raw skill, the results are driven by the comfort level of dealing with pressure. That is why poker players and gunfighters go hand and hand with business. Because in all reality, it's all the same game.

CHAPTER NOTES:

a. Most business people play a kind of poker game with house money to play the cards best that we are dealt with.
b. Their goal is to place bets to maximize the chances of winning before the river card is revealed.
c. The natural risk-takers understand how to manage those conditions even when the hands at play aren't very good.
d. The poker game requires players to manage pressure well; whether bluffing, holding tight on a good hand, or folding, it is how the round is played with calm, collected thoughts that bring about the most victories.

SCAM OF THE BOUNTY HUNTERS

It is truly something to behold how many companies purchase the advice of consultants these days when the information needed is already in front of everyone. The gimmicks of consultants come into a business enterprise of some kind and utilize some snake oil potion to convince those paying that suddenly their life will improve as a business. They will then be more competitive in the marketplace. Thinking of these "consultants" in the way themed in this book, these characters are the bounty hunters of our focus. It used to be in the early days of frontier life that the law representatives didn't have the courage or resources to solve their problems, so they'd hire bounty hunters to resolve things for them.

Particularly in America, hiring bounty hunters to solve company problems has been way too familiar in our modern time. The reason is the lack of leadership that is essentially part of our daily life. The bounty hunters make their livings off the timidity typical business management displays to solve the complex problems before them so that someone else can be the responsible change agent. Much like a local sheriff might have feared eliminating a dangerous criminal, it was much easier for them to hire someone else to deal with it. And if things did go wrong, there would be someone else to blame. Thus, that is how business consultants have infected our modern industry. If there were leadership and courage already present, companies could take care of business challenges themselves. After all, anyone could carry a gun and resolve a dangerous situation on their own. Anyone can pick up a few books and begin to apply some thoughts to a complicated problem in business. But what is lacking is courage and a dedication to personal responsibility, so the desire is to hire the bounty hunter to come in and tell everyone what they already know. The benefit is that the people doing the hiring don't have to get their own hands dirty.

This elusive problem has set the stage for many different ideas to come into play from other cultures due to the nature of bounty hunters, which would be good if diversity in understanding is the goal. After all, bounty hunters aren't concerned about what happens to a company after its services are rendered. They only care that they get paid, and they are enormously expensive. Much of what they end up doing for a company could have been done by anybody. Everyone knows where the bad guys live and what must be done to resolve a business. But they take a back seat to the resolution due to their fears of getting involved and overstepping their station in the work culture. It is easier for the current management failures to allow some outside miracle worker to justify why it was too dangerous for ordinary people to solve a series of complex problems. It would, after all, prevent up-and-coming ladder climbers from outshining managers who made all the mistakes to begin with. Many of the concepts of great productivity started in North America. These days, we find ourselves hindered by so much regulation and sensitivity that hiring outside bounty hunters has been much easier than dealing with the problems themselves. In this way, bounty hunters, "consultants" have injected a lot of Eastern thinking into our uniquely Western culture. The results last as long as the bounty hunters are present but usually don't stick due to the nature of the work culture. Bounty hunters bring their tricks and gimmicks to unite employees around solutions that they could have done themselves if they had the courage or freedom to act—whether self-imposed or company mandated. After all, if things go wrong, it is much easier to blame the bounty hunter. But if things go right, everyone can admit that it took outside help to resolve the matter. Admitting the actual failures of a company and its lack of leadership requires a self-analysis that most aren't willing to embark. That is why the bounty hunters come, and they come from other mysterious cultures much of the time.

The method of selling these unique viewpoints is through consensus building, in which the bounty hunters need to perform many of their magic tricks and is part of the show that is purchased. However, what is exhibited is the lack of leadership which led to the bounty hunters in the first place. To sell that, the bounty hunter has to allow the people to believe that future sustainability will be possible through teamwork and by following their magical boons. What is ignored is that the targeted villain or villains of the endeavor may have just been harmless reprobates who had been suckling off the chaos inherent of an organization due to the failure to deal with good people, and bad people are always present. The bounty hunter, through some theatrical ritual, may bring in the head of a known threat and then show everyone how to defend from such a menace in the future by orienting the stage-coaches in a circle when camping for the night or teaching people how to shoot a gun to protect themselves. Still, that power had always been in work culture if only leadership had recognized the need and done something about it on their own.

The tendency to hire a bounty hunter to resolve problems is the same one that believes intelligence and leadership can be purchased instead of being earned through hard work and merit. People who lack courage and leadership find it comforting to know that whatever they need to solve a problem can be purchased if only they throw enough money in that direction. When they look at their books and all their numbers are upside down, they can hire a bounty hunter to make everything right. That is also why when the bounty hunter leaves, the work culture snaps right back into the elements that put everyone in danger before. What was purchased with the money was a temporary fix, and the bounty hunters know it. That's why they camp on the edge of town and wait for a call to return. That's how they make their money. They depend on the lack of courage and personal responsibility that is the tendency of most of their dealings, and they get very wealthy off exposing that weakness.

Just as a bounty hunter may have eliminated some murderer in times past from peace-loving farmers who didn't have it in their nature to take up arms, the bounty hunter is a hired gun that allows for guilt-free relief. They take action from those paying. And when the menace is eliminated, people can go back to doing what they were doing until the successive crises comes again. However, life isn't happily ever after due to the failure to deal with the real problem, the lack of leadership that caused the villains to appear in the first place. While the bounty hunter may eliminate one, another will come along, and the bounty hunter never really wants to solve the problem. Bounty hunters want to be wanted, so they'll never desire to solve the real issues. With all their advice and all their tricks, they never address the real problem. If they did, everyone would figure out that the bounty hunters were never really needed and that the solutions were always accessible for any business to obtain independently. The real threats to them were not the drunken criminal or the black-hatted gunfighters who come to town with chaos at their backs to destroy all they can get their hands on just for the thrill of it. The real threat was their lack of courage to face the troubles in front of them and falling to the temptation to let someone else deal with it.

CHAPTER NOTES:

a. The temptation of hiring consultants, called bounty hunters here, allows a company to mitigate the risk of a bad decision while looking for solutions to elusive problems.
b. Bounty hunters make their living off the fear of risk in invoking a change agency.
c. The need for bounty hunters is created due to a lack of courage and leadership in business culture. Bounty hunters generally inject tricks and gimmicks picked up from eastern cultures that are exotic to the environments in question. Courage can't be genuinely purchased.
d. Bounty hunters only care to get paid; they do not care about future sustainability. Once their job is done, they reside in the shadows and wait for the calls to come again. That's how they make their money.

EDUCATION AND THE SNAKE OIL BANDITS

Of course, education in business is a tremendous asset. Yet, in the times of some of the most remarkable creations and expansions of wealth in America, many of the participants were not what we might call "educated." Many of them had difficulty reading and didn't finish grade school past the third grade. Those days, the people we called gunfighters were not pouring out of the university system and becoming industry titans. Yet many of them are the ones we remember in history for their bold, often rambunctious behavior and their antics of self-destruction, such as Wyatt Earp. People know that name more universally than they do Alfred P. Sloan and draw inspiration by the bold shootout at the O.K. Corral. Sure, business insiders know of Sloan and the MIT Sloan School of Management at Cambridge. But when it comes down to it, which is the better example of leadership and, therefore, the one they would follow under tenuous conditions? The answer is audaciously clear. There have been many movies and books written about Wyatt Earp, but very little in mainstream culture said about a CEO at General Motors during the 1930s when the car industry experienced some of its most creative years. Education is a good thing. They do an excellent job at MIT and other teaching scenario-based exchanges that can take a mid-level career and put them into executive positions effectively. But the education itself won't make those executives great; it's what they do in their life that people end up following.

Education is fine, but that is not what people follow, and any manager or executive leading an organization must deal with this problem. People don't follow academics; they follow people who have experience and know what's going on. Education alone can't purchase respect, so we must deal with this subject with some deconstruction. Our society has been built on the false premise that education is the key to success. It is not. Much of the wealth that built up New York City or placed the railroads across America were not from scholars of note; they were much like the gunfighters of the time. Hard, battle-formed people such as Cornelius Vanderbilt. Rugged people of Western Expansion in the saloons and shootouts of smoke-filled rooms with the genius of American capitalism—ambition and nobody but courage standing in the way of achieving it. Two fists and a refusal to yield to circumstances are the molds that made America and the wealth creation so popular within it, which exploded with influence.

The morality of our times has indicated that it is teamwork that makes success or failure. This isn't true; it is a concept invented by academics to loot off the boldness of the job creators and sell a product their institutions could manage from a classroom's safe distance. Whether it be the free government schools that most of our culture navigates as a young person or an advanced college degree, the goal of those institutions is not to make a better individual or even a leader. Their goal is to create a compliant teammate and mold the individual into a collective-based thinker for service to the organization.

The truth is that the schools of any kind miss the mark entirely; in fact, they aren't even at the target range to even see what they are trying to shoot. The myth of education is that in exchange for some money paid, the result will be more intelligence that will cause others to follow you. And that isn't what people follow. There is a term I like to use a lot in my exchanges, especially when the "teamwork" word is tossed around as loosely as it commonly is, "there is no I in team, but there is in win." The harsh reality of our times is that teams don't win much of anything. It's always a bold individual that people follow who does. Whether the example is a sports story or a significant mover and shaker in the industry, a leader must do something spectacular. A team of people follows a leader to victory; a team is not a democracy of equals. The team doesn't do the strategic thinking that creates success; they do the work—they are meant to follow a leader. If a leader isn't built within an organization or utilized in some ambitious way, a team is just a collection of people waiting around for someone to follow.

Most of our education institutes throw around the word leadership as if it's something they give out with the price of their courses. Still, in all honesty, leaders are made somewhere else and under different conditions. Others don't make leaders, they make themselves, so it's very much an individualized pursuit. Under capitalism and within a few short years of the Civil War, and the shackles were taken off the human mind for the first time in world history, the magic of innovation and wealth creation bloomed. Before Sloan gave MIT a grant to create the School of Industrial Management, gunfighters and poker games laid out the foundation for the explosive economic growth that essentially put the nation to work, and it wasn't teams that did it. It was bold and reckless individuals who put their fears aside to create something that the world had never seen before. That's what people followed under their employment.

Even today, many years bridging over the history of the last hundred- and forty-years business owners and top executives are naturally on the reckless side, they must be. It is hard for them to turn off what made them great to begin with. Once they've tasted some success, that same riverboat gambler and metaphorical gunslinger in them that climbed way out on a limb to build their business is the same one that has to fend off all the boot lickers that come after. Wild stories of overconsumption follow them, whether they are crazy relationships with the opposite sex or drinking too much. The best in the business industry is not the clean-cut graduates of MIT; they are much closer in life experience to Wyatt Earp and Doc Holliday, living on the edge and willing to face down a bullet without flinching.

Despicably, that is not the goal of any of our education systems, not even in the military. The teaching of our day has been built off assumptions by academics looking for an entry point they could sell to students that let them hide their natures from the mandate of courage that is always required. They used teamwork to disguise their anxieties, which is fine for people not so inclined to boldness. Yet you can't hide the fact that people follow leaders and not team members. Without a leader or someone willing to walk into a gunfight, metaphorical or literal, and face down danger without fear, nothing advances. Corporations remain in a static state. Small businesses flounder on the periphery of existence. The parasites, boot lickers, and other brownnosers nestle up to the strong and call it teamwork. That was how they were taught from grade school of how it was in the world, which of course, they were wrong.

CHAPTER NOTES:

a. In the most expansive examples of wealth building, the best and boldest enterprises were not coming out of the education systems.
b. People do not follow people's titles acquired through education. Education won't make people follow leaders.
c. Teamwork was a device created by academics to loot off the efforts of leaders. There is no "I" in team, but there is in "win."
d. The team follows a leader to victory. The leader does the thinking that delivers the win. Leaders are made under pressure and experience; the skill can't be purchased.

THE TYRANNY OF SAFETY

One thing about business that doesn't get talked about much but is an increasing concern is the compliance culture driven partly by the government, mainly by supply chain competition, and ultimately the insurance industry. In this culture, safety and references become a hidden tyrant that seeks to control your business and quickly be overrun by any of those contributors mentioned during an audit process. A cut finger here, a sprained back, isn't just a concern for losing employees to lost time. Many regulatory factors exist for those so-called employees politically. Once hurt, these regulators sweep in to take away management ability for those employees, leaving your business with little to do but comply. Of course, this leads to the natural reaction to treat every situation with many restrictions on productivity. This is the aim of many auditors who visit your facility, all in the name of "safety." What it comes down to is power, power for them at your company's expense. What is often unknown in these escapades is that large companies essentially run these safety initiatives. They seek to put their rivals out of business with the cost of compliance and heavy regulation. They can then use their power to leverage pricing within their supply chains. That makes this whole compliance business a significant concern for any business struggling to make a profit to operate under. The challenges to delivering their products to market are intense by themselves. But when all this compliance is considered, the task is daunting and unprofitable.

Naturally, the amount of regulatory burden out there is nearly impossible to fill for any company. Most cannot afford a team of professionals to protect them from this element, so there is great fear about the amount of power many auditors have over the company and its employees. I have always seen the situation as a band of bandits who take over a town with the desire of extorting money from the defenseless and defending their evil by calling the payments for the company's good. That is no different than some black-hatted figure riding into a Wild West town and kicking over a few tables, and harassing people with a proposal of violence, then telling everyone that if only they paid this much money, that they'd just go away. But until they do pay, they aren't leaving.

We have all come to understand how companies work if, on paper, you have a dangerous workplace because statistically, by employee population, if you exceed whatever quota they have for your population, your insurance rates will go up. Connected to these aggressive actions are the government and a peer group regulatory class looking for every opportunity to levy a fee for every injury that happens to an employee. Then there are the doctors themselves, who then take over the management of your employees with the stroke of a pen. Once an employee is injured, your company essentially loses control of your internal management of that employee until the doctor decides that you get them back. The federal government uses regulations to behave as terrorists toward capitalism, all in the name of "safety."

The first thing you must learn about the "safety and compliance" culture in the modern world is that what they are doing is not about safety. For many centuries hard-working people have pulled muscles, cut fingers, and generally found themselves in dangerous conditions. However, what the safety culture seeks to do is to put themselves between the employees of an employer and gain control of that part of management, significantly weakening the relationship the company has with its employees. This presents enormous detriments in building teams and creating a positive "can do" work culture. Safety terrorists are always roaming around looking for a legal excuse to penalize a company for noncompliance. A quick look at the typical members of these terrorist marauders shows that they are typically weak and fearful people. They seek to alleviate those fears by enforcing group-oriented compliance, giving them a sense of meaning in their otherwise meaningless lives.

The best thing that managers and owners can do to protect their company from these elements is to think about their role as a gunfighter who might approach those marauders in the street under occupation and eliminate them from concern. No fear can be shown because the safety marauders will detect such a thing and feed off it. If they smell fear on you, they will pounce in their audits and seek to take as much money as they can legally confiscate through fines. In dealing with them, you must understand their intentions and remove their leverage from your operations.

Working with guns naturally helps anybody learn to be safer. When a gunfighter handles a gun and conducts all the practices it takes to become proficient at a competitive level, that same mind then carries over into other things. People who are around guns a lot and learn to use them without causing injury to themselves are also the same people who get hurt less often and know not to panic over every little thing because they are accustomed to danger. Becoming comfortable with risk is a key to staying out of trouble when opportunities for injury do occur. Again, it's not that we bring guns to compliance audits, but we do get a lack of fear. And to keep the compliance audits minimal and conduct a safer workplace, the more people in your business who understand the handling of guns, the smoother they will be under pressure in the events that cause accidents. The solution to the whole enterprise is as a business representative. A lack of fear is present to minimize the occurrences and push away the compliance parasites that come after to loot whatever money they can manage in the wake of tragedy. Avoiding tragedy is the best thing. The path to outstanding safety records isn't more government or audits but in individuals conducting themselves safely by overcoming many fears that lead to unsafe behavior.

As managers and owners working with guns and conducting life in a way where you are comfortable with danger will prepare your mind in dealing with safety terrorists who thrive off fear to extract the money they seek to loot off companies, all in the name of the greater good. When you do not fear them and know that you can defend yourself from anything they might throw at you, you will have less anxiety about their visits, creating fear in the business toward their arrival. As a bonus, encouraging employees to spend their leisure time doing dangerous things will make them safer because they will be more prepared for danger when it does show. Fewer injuries will ultimately minimize the opportunities for those compliance audits to extract fees during their visits because there will be a minimal audit. You must be fearless by living your life in a way that teaches you to be comfortable with danger. Spend your leisure shooting guns, riding roller coasters, and perhaps driving 10 to 20 miles over the speed limit. In those small ways, fear management will make those audits a lot more manageable.

CHAPTER NOTES:

a. A compliant culture intends to allow regulators to sweep in and take away management control in a facility. It's all about power and control.
b. The compliance culture is similar to a band of hijackers holding hostage something of value unless a specific price is paid. It's a scam of a different kind to rob from the productive and give to the parasites.
c. The best things that a manager can do are think like a gunfighter, develop a fearless attitude toward audits, and remove the leverage of auditors from your operations.
d. Shooting at a gun range can settle the nerves and help a work culture become comfortable with risk. Under pressure in the workplace, people will behave more safely, taking away the potential for leverage from compliance parasites. Be fearless and comfortable with danger to manage the stress of an audit.

THE DANGER OF A HALFCOCKED AMBUSH

It is incredible how much terminology we use every day from the American period of the gunfighter and the games of poker that went with their lifestyle. Examples such as "all in" and "don't go off halfcocked" permeate our daily conversations, and in most situations, we have forgotten their origins. But innately, we understand their meanings and how they apply to whatever references we are making. Speaking specifically of the term "halfcocked," I spent years saying it without really understanding it. It had an implication of recklessness, so it seemed to fit, but the real meaning of the term didn't come alive for me until I joined the Cowboy Fast Draw Association and started learning that new skill. I stay focused when undergoing business activities, especially ones with a lot of pressure, because I shoot at a target range. During one challenging project, I needed to shoot every day, so I joined Cowboy Fast Draw and bought one of their targeting systems that have timed light mechanisms that measure the speed of a fast draw. It is in this development that I learned why the term halfcocked was such a wise warning.

The game of fast draw with actual .45 caliber single-action revolvers has many suitable lessons to help a strategic mind toward its objectives. The Cowboy Fast Draw Association does a great job providing excellent equipment to work with on a very professional level. Their targeting systems are essentially various metal plates with a light in the center that indicates that it's time to draw. A digital clock measures how fast you can draw your gun and fire a wax bullet that impacts the target plate from various distances. Everything is very safe if done correctly.

The wax bullets make it so that you can do all this in the comfort of your garage, which is why I selected it as a hobby for this particular project that had massive international implications. The pressure was very intense, so learning a new skill that involved shooting helped put my mind in the right place to do the job.

With this targeting system, I learned to balance out the various pressures involved in Cowboy Fast Draw. The goal is speed and accuracy, but how fast and accurate quickly becomes the dominating factor during practice. I often found that to improve my times and get the gun out of the holster fast, I would halfcock the gun often. In Cowboy Fast Draw, you stand on a line setting the distance, and position yourself for the shot. The light on the target blinks three times, letting you know to be ready. There is a slight pause composed of various lengths so that you cannot know when the light will come on. Then the light comes on solid, not flashing, and your time is in your reaction to it. In my first few months of this activity, I was getting times in the .600 of a second range, meaning just over half a second.

While you are waiting for the light to come on, you are allowed as the shooter to put your shooting hand on the gun in what they called a "lawmen ready" position. But the gun must still be in your holster. The trick is that you have to cock the gun, insert your trigger finger into the trigger guard, and lay down a shot right after the gun has cleared the holster and can be pointed at the target. Good times, which I get now, are in the .300 of a second range. But getting there, I found that I was "halfcocking" the gun a lot. I was so focused on getting the gun on target quickly that I didn't give enough attention to actually cocking the hammer back all the way. It's an easy mistake to happen because, at speeds that fast with so many steps, it's effortless to shorten one into ineffectiveness.

Fast draw shooting gave new meaning to the term "halfcocked" because you could imagine some gunfighter putting their life on the line in a dual with a challenger and pushing themselves to be the fastest on the draw for obvious reasons. If they lost the dual, there wouldn't be a second chance. These were the conditions when "halfcocking" became a real problem. Even though they might beat their rival to the draw, they wouldn't get their gun cocked in time because their thumb on a single action pistol wouldn't have pushed the hammer back far enough, leaving the gun in a position not to fire. The whole management of avoiding a "halfcock" is essentially a lesson on stress management. Learning to avoid the "halfcock" in Cowboy Fast Draw is an invaluable tool of stress management in all things in life. I have found that it works exceptionally well in putting your mind in the right place for tenuous conditions. Golf, in many ways, does too, as do many sports. But they are working with a gun in conditions under a second forces, quick decisions, and a level of calm in the middle of the storm that can come from few other places. And let's face it, most decisions in management, especially at the executive level, need to be fast and relentless.

Just because a term or a practice comes from a time that has been long forgotten, the lessons from those events can sometimes be better than the applications of the modern age. Just because new practices are current with their terminology doesn't make them better, and I found that going back to some of our American traditions helped train my mind for the very current pressures of modern business. Learning to think fast and accurately helps tremendously, and there are few sports in the world that force such fast thinking and action. The key to surviving some of those tough business decisions that come to everyone, and can be crushing to the spirit, is training your mind to function well under pressure. Many businesspeople fail when the pressure gets to them and end up "halfcocked" in their efforts. They may show up to close the big deal, or they may have all their production requirements lined up and ready to kill. But when it comes to hitting the target, whether it is in sustaining the close of a significant customer or in hitting the target objectives, likely cost-related, if the effort fails, then what's the point in trying? You may beat your rivals to the shot, but if your gun isn't cocked, you are going to lose to the slower person who was more methodical and arrived with a cocked weapon.

Yet, that is not an excuse to go slow. Initially, my original times were .600 of a second, and after many thousands of shots, they are now in the .300s. What used to be very fast is now very slow, so the skill level is undoubtedly a measuring factor. When an executive says that they need more time, what they are saying is that they aren't fast enough for the task. A rival who is fast enough will beat them, and that is the way of things. So while this warning about not going off halfcocked is a measurable concern, it's not an excuse for those who don't have the skill to shoot fast and accurately. If you don't have the skills today, the message is that you better practice and get them because the objective conditions are indicators of the demand. The demand does not care if you don't have the skill to obtain it. It's up to you to make yourself able to accomplish the task through practice, and sound, productive thought, and the perspective of stress management under the most tenuous conditions.

CHAPTER NOTES:

a. Halfcocked is a term that runs deep in our culture, most of us say it all the time, and it can be managed best by practicing with firearms.
b. Pressure to perform under great expectation brings about the temptation to pull a gun out of the holster too fast, not properly pulling back the hammer all the way.
c. The necessity of drawing a gun under timed pressure teaches how to manage speed and accuracy without sacrificing the steps of the process, and this can be applied directly to business management.
d. It doesn't do any good to draw a gun faster than the other fighter if the gun isn't cocked. But you can't take all day either. Speed is as important as accuracy and must be practiced so that both aspects of management can come to the light of day under pressure.

CARD GAMES OF GUNFIGHTERS AND MYSTICS

There has always been an undercurrent to voodoo and black magic that has permeated the antics of Western Expansion. The slave culture of the South mixed with European Catholicism turned the game of Tarot cards into a mystical fortune reading endeavor that filled the corners of every civilized outpost from the Atlantic coast to the Pacific. As the Civil War closed and the South and North moved West to fill the land openings available, these games and their mystic assumptions went with them. And that was certainly the case in New Orleans, where poker was refined toward the American sensibilities along the Mississippi River during the formation of the new country. Both renditions of past-time banter involved cards and a glimpse into the life patterns revealed in the games. When it came to the Tarot, the cards told stories of a person's past, current state, and future. However, the game's goals were much more decisive; the goal was to play the cards to win—not allowing the cards to determine the winner.

The roots of these approaches to mysterious elements are still very much a part of present-day business. Even now, many top executives with all the statistical information at their disposal essentially resort to Tarot cards and voodoo to determine what comes next in their plans. And poker still proves to be a game for the winners who know how to push up a pot and then capitalize on the weaknesses of others to bring home the goods. The apparent difference between the two is that one version of those card games assumes that fate is already established and that to follow it best, we need some guide of supernatural guidance, where the stars are aligned a certain way. Certain things will happen, as opposed to the self-determination of playing fate for the gains of the individual.

It is not uncommon for top management to tap on a desktop and declare, "knock on wood." It's a superstition as if to suggest good fortune might be robbed away by chance at any moment. Fate might be altered just for mentioning the word "good" in public. The same gods and spirits clamored to in the Tarot might become angry and bestow lousy luck on everyone involved if appeasement is not the diet of the declaration. The gods, after all, as everyone knows, expect appeasement and sacrifice. What would anybody be willing to sacrifice for success? Those beliefs, as archaic as they sound, are the everyday business practices of some of America's best these days, and their roots go back way in time to the mystics who claimed to control such forces for the price of a small fee. Many on the early frontiers of America would find some fortune teller wagon traveling along the popular trade routes and find the mystic there who would do a palm reading or a fortune-telling through the cards—and they'd believe the result.

Typically, however, among the gunfighters was a belief that their sheer will controlled chance. That is why poker became such a popular game during this period. Even though when wrong hands turn up, "luck" is often treated as a fateful representative; the game aims to control the situation no matter what cards you may have, leaving fate up to the player, not played by the mystic. This essential distinction is the difference between success and failure in life. Leaving the great games in life to random chance and fate is the sure sign of disappointments.

All across this nation and the world right now are business calls up and down a supply chain where excuses are abundant, such as we can't do this or that because we don't have a second or third shift. We have all our prominent people out on vacation, or even yet, our supplier couldn't supply us. Circumstantial blame is the main focus of the task. Many people function in the business world and essentially run their lives off the same methodology as a Tarot card reading by some frontier mystic. Sometimes random chance does occur, and good things happen even when they weren't planned. That is certainly the case with bad things. But looking to the cards for guidance is as foolish as just closing your eyes and pointing in a direction and hoping to find gold by walking in whatever random direction you choose.

The way to win at business is the same as it is in poker. You may have a bad hand, but you can play it to good results; it depends on your skill in manipulating others at the table. And if they don't bite, then how well you recover on the future rounds. On average, the goal is to empty them and fill yourself. However, you don't always want to do that on the opening rounds. The purpose of poker isn't always to win. Sometimes you want to lose so that you can win and encourage other players to put more of their money in the pot. The difference between the gunfighter and the mystic looks to supernatural aid to navigate life, the gunfighter on their wits and skill. That is also why Tarot cards in American culture are not and will never be a mainstream thing, but poker is. Poker is broadcast on television as many people find it interesting enough to watch as a spectator sport. They don't understand why. They are drawn to it due to the truth of the game in how it relates to their reality.

Gunfighters have a reputation for recklessness and courage, but what they all have in common is that they don't typically look to the cards to tell them how to live their life. Instead, they look to the cards to take advantage for themselves against the tides of universal conduct that often has roots in the mysterious and sublime. As human beings, we have invented card games to touch the elements of life that our senses aren't designed to detect, and two schools of thought have emerged in how to deal with them. One is the mystic approach of letting the cards determine the reality of the curious. The other is in the instigator, using the cards to define reality to their advantage. Both involve cards of marginal usefulness, only in the symbols printed on them. It is the mind that is drawn to the results created within the context of the game. The two approaches are broken down into all life forms and how the consumer views all of existence. For the successful to be so, they play poker or at least some symbolic version to make gains for themselves and those who depend on them. They control even their bad hands and find ways to benefit from every circumstance, no matter how bad it may be. They don't shake their fist at the sky and cry injustice when things go wrong. They simply look at their cards, measure them against their competitor, and then decide to fold, check, or push up the bets—but they are always in control.

CHAPTER NOTES:

a. Our card games reflect two types of approaches to management; Tarot cards reveal a superstitious approach, whereas poker takes ownership of making the best of what the dealer deals.
b. Gunfighter's believed in the sheer will of controlled chance, which is why poker was the card game preferred by them. Fate was up to the player.
c. Too much decision-making in business is dedicated to circumstantial blame, the same mentality that equated to frontier mystics allowing cards to determine success.
d. The purpose of poker isn't always to win, sometimes by losing, you win because it pushes fate into a way that favors recklessness and courage, which runs against the sublime of universal circumstance.

IT'S BETTER TO BE A GHOST

One truth in the universe that is absolute is that people will talk no matter who or what station in life they reside. Even among the best of friends, gossip and jealous utterances will permeate discussions. From the beginning of time to the last person on earth, gossip will be one of the most corrosive forces contributing to the most conversation. As discovered by early American gunfighters, the good strategist was to control much of that talk by giving them all something to talk about. After all, if they are talking about you, you influence where the conversation is going. You can use that toward a business advantage in our modern times. I refer to this behavior as "ghosting it." Being a ghost in the minds of the many. Even when you aren't there, people are thinking about you.

Ghosts are interesting because they can travel through time and space, move through walls, and get to all locked places once they take hold of the imaginations of the masses. It wasn't that uncommon to have a duel with a rival in the times of what we call the Old West. Dueling was outlawed after the Revolutionary War, but it was still widespread, especially in the antebellum south. As the Civil War came to a close, the dueling culture was still very much on people's minds, especially on the open frontier where there may not have been any legal presence for hundreds and hundreds of miles. When a dispute overflowed beyond a fistfight, a gunfight was a sentiment expected and brought about many of the myths that we have today about real gunfighters living and dying by the point of a gun. Yet many of those gunfights weren't as spectacular as people remembered them; often, it was two very scared or very drunk people who faced off on a dusty street or a back alley somewhere and fought to the death without really thinking of the long-term consequences. At the moment of the gunfight, the heroics were nowhere near as epic as people remembered it, but the exchange of stories cascaded from those events brought legendary consequences. If the gunfighter was a short, dumpy, balding fellow, by the time the winner of the fight was talked about from town to town, he was 7-foot-tall and faster than a snake. People speak and remember events magnificently, leaving the ghost of memory more valuable than the actual event.

In our present time, a lot of wasted effort is spent trying to control what people say about you by being nice to them and making friends. That is a wasted effort. Even the best friend in the world will stick a knife in your back when others are around. They will tell stories that are a very negative reflection of your conduct, so being nice to anybody just for the sake of winning favor is not an intelligent use of time. If you will be nice to someone, do it because you want to and are good. Not so you can leverage future gains through the friendship. Instead, don't worry about what people say positive or negative, about you. It is irrelevant to worry. The best approach is to know that people will be looking for something to talk about regarding anybody. That is the way of people, and the best thing in their lives is watching what others do. So if you find that you need to control the flow of information through them, give them what they want most. Everyone likes to be afraid of ghosts, phantoms of imagination, and the all-seeing context of legend.

The most successful gunfighters, such as Bat Masterson and Luke Short knew how to approach a dual. Of course, there were always risks, but if a person survived the fight, the people watching would talk about what a great event it was, and the winner would be cast into the forges of mythology forever. Just like in the great game of poker, if you found yourself facing down some loser with a gun, terrified, drunk, inexperienced, if you were skilled, you were likely going to win by holding the best deck. So playing out the action with a bit of fanfare to let people's imaginations run wild in the aftermath wasn't a bad thing. It was equivalent to pushing a pile of chips into the pot to go for a big win in such fights. Chances were good that you'd win the fight, so you might as well make it look good so that the gossip would make a legend out of you. Then, even when you aren't there, people will claim that you appeared as a mistlike ghost and moved through a wall, knowing their every action and know that you can hear every word, even if physically you are on the other side of the world. Ghosts exist in the mind of the guilty and treacherous, and their effect is driven by imagination and can be the greatest weapon of an all-seeing manager.

Today is no different in business; fights of other kinds are commonplace. They are now conducted with emails and handshakes, but the goals aren't much different if you peel away enough of the décor. People will talk poorly about you even if you do the best job in the world. You can take them to dinner; you can go golfing with them. You can donate countless amounts of money to their charities. They will still talk bad about you when you aren't around if there is a conduit to provoke the discussion, and with rivals always on the horizon, there are conduits. Knowing that, give them something to talk about that you control, so in that way, you are at least holding their minds in some indirect way. If you know that they will be talking, then provide the content. Even if it is harmful because they will have elevated your reputation in the minds by the time they are done, making it much easier to have those hard conversations with those who need motivations from a competent manager.

The rumor mill is one of the most corrosive elements of any professional endeavor. But rather than fight that trait in people, use it to your advantage. Know that everything you say and do and gossip about what you do in your personal life will trickle back to some water-cooler conversation about you so that when you walk by, and everyone gets quiet, you will know that you have a place in all their minds that commands their actions. Knowing that in themselves, they will find an uncontrollable desire to appease you due to the betrayal they know they participated in, and they will work much harder for you due to that fact alone. The same works for good deeds as well; if you do a little bit nice for a person, they will talk about it, and soon you will be known as a person of great justice and fairness, when in reality, what you may have done was just a little thing.

If there is one thing that you can trust in this world, people almost more than anything love to gossip and talk about other people. They do it within their own families, they do it about their neighbors, and they certainly do it among their co-workers. Even husbands and wives and best forever friends find the temptation to gossip about the people closest to them insatiable. They can't help it, and I have yet to find a management method from any of the bounty hunters out there who have put their finger on this human trait effectively. Most of the time, if they deal with it, the proposal is always some consensus driver that works counterintuitive to human nature. People pay lip service to the technique, but they don't invest because what they want out of their exchange with other people is to roll in the glutton of gossip that always comes with relationships. Don't allow the thought of how you'd like the world to behave to create illusions about the way it is. Instead, endeavor to be a ghost, to be everpresent in the minds of those you deal with. You will find that it is a much more powerful position than in being seen in your office or the front of a boardroom—or anywhere people can consolidate to themselves that you are just as much as flesh and blood as they are—which of course, they don't want.

CHAPTER NOTES:

a. People will talk no matter what level of society they reside in; gossip is one of the most corrosive forces in the universe. So why not control what people talk about.
b. Ghosting refers to inspiring the natural inclinations of people to gossip. Ghosts travel through walls, time, and space, and they reside in the imaginations of people. Being a ghost is more powerful than residing in a physical form because the ghost can live in people's minds and have much more influence.
c. Do not be nice to people to control what they say and think about you because it controls a situation in their favor and away from you. Don't try to leverage gains through friendships.
d. Give people something to talk about; what people want most is to gossip about something. Provide the content that puts the situation back in your hands.

WHEN THE DANDIES COME LOOTING

I've always had an appreciation of Wild West Towns; the image of them was always about hope and growth as humankind put up a few rickety buildings on a wild frontier to become something great. In the early days of town development, well before any law presence was formed, it was just the honor between people that kept order and when it didn't, the morality of the gun. Some towns succeeded, and most failed to become what we call ghost towns. Those who did thrive and continued to grow beyond the formation of a bank, a saloon, and a mortuary came the big city dandies. They came looking for a wave to ride in on and lay claims to some success once the hard work of forming the town was done.

Wild West Towns and most modern businesses are the same essential thing. They have in common the efforts of capitalism to drive their growth; where New York, Cincinnati, and St. Louis went from towns to cities in a reasonably short time, most companies follow the same trajectory. In the beginning, there are always stories of bold individuals who fight against all odds to create something from nothing. Then once something is made, there is always a culture of dandies hanging out on the outskirts waiting to claim jump on the opportunities created from the bold efforts of capitalism. Like big cities, all large corporations started from some humble beginnings. Once the die had been cast, the dandies then take over the management, bringing with them cultures of appearance over substance and emphasizing style instead of results.

The upward trajectory of any endeavor is always started by the bold individuals who began the enterprise. Still, once they have done their work, the dandies ride that wave before a gradual decline, and the effort becomes apparent, and their eventual deaths are evident to anybody who knows what to look for. Countless modern examples present themselves as evidence. The dandies lacked the courage to create, but in many cases, they can manage to sustain some level of growth once the formula for success has been spelled out for them. They are the natural parasites of humankind and do have their role. But what they do is never as exciting as that first start-up with the "can do" spirit of a few shacks and a lot of hope that usually are the fuel of any start-up enterprise.

Yet, it is always the dandies who are the ones who must call the bounty hunters to deal with threats in the future because they don't have the heart to create anything. Their history was in the shadows waiting for the bold gunslingers to do the work of taming an endeavor from the primal demands of nature. Then to mask their natural anxieties and reluctance toward courage, they come up with dress codes and laws of regulatory conduct to lay claim to their inventiveness. And that is their first mistake, as cities like Detroit provide witness testimony. The boom times are easy, the natural output of what the bold created. The wave of success only lasts so long before more courage is needed from a leadership standpoint to bring order and production to an endeavor. That is when the dandies call the bounty hunters to help where their weaknesses prevent decisive action. However, the bounty hunters do not care about the endeavor; they want to get paid, so they do the job asked of them, but the culture that created the problems remains intact, making the original issue a reoccurring one. When the dandies run out of money, they tend to move on to some other claim jump, and the endeavor then dies a slow death, like the city of Detroit did in modern America.

It may seem we are talking about two things here when we are only talking about one, the creation of towns and businesses, how they decline, and what creates that condition. There will always be dandies in government and dandies in industry. Once they feel safe, they come on the scene and then loot off the bold efforts before them created. If they come in too soon, they can kill a project before it ever gets off the ground. Because dandies only really care about appearances, they do not know what makes something work on the epistemological level.

Dandies will always be a fact of life; college fraternities and sororities are filled with them, which can be a necessary evil. In the best examples, they can help continue growth in a company so long as they create a bold and courageous path to continue innovating. I'm thinking of Kelly Johnson at the great company Lockheed Martin. He came in as an underlying engineer and ended up saving the company and taking it to the next level of business as many learned that it was wise to follow after him. It is possible in a Dandie culture to continue to innovate so long as the style seekers continue to take a back seat to the bold and courageous. They teach many things in the Dandies' culture, most of them relating to the appearance of things, which is just fine so long as impressions don't get in the way of results.

It all comes down to someone must be able to pull the trigger on ideas and concepts, unifying efforts behind brash heroism; otherwise, growth does not happen. Whether the endeavor is a Wild West Town in North America, prosperity carries it into a city under excellent care and individual boldness. Or a significant corporation starting in someone's garage, the needs are the same; someone has to be willing to face down the villains that want to prevent growth from happening, or instead want to loot off it for their gains and everyone else's detriment.

Is it that simple? Well yes. The essence of things may conceal itself behind the antics of the many dandies that live in our world. They may have claim jumped boldness over the many years of our observation. But the truth cannot be denied. The gunfighters of the early towns made it possible for growth due to their reckless courage. In cases where a city had enough time to sink roots into a sustaining industry, it kept the temptations toward primitive reckonings away for the time needed. Such is the business case; it takes the bold, the reckless, and the ambitious to make something from nothing. The dandies come in later and lay claim to the efforts, which everyone sees once an endeavor becomes large. However, it was never the dandies who created anything, and by nature, they never will. At best, they can sustain what was created. But they do not have the guts to make it or remake it if the effort somehow becomes lost. For the creation, the world must always turn to the gunslingers.

CHAPTER NOTES:

a. The dandies are the come lately types who tend to claim-jump the work of those who pave the way with hard work and risk.
b. Dandies tend to help carry on a growth period that is always born from the ambitions of a start-up enterprise.
c. The food of the dandies is regulatory conduct because it disguises their timidity, which is the first step toward the decline of any culture.
d. Gunslingers and dandies are not natural allies. They are both valid, but they will never share common ground philosophically. They can only work together if the culture can still embrace the danger and recklessness of the gunslingers and doesn't end up choked out by the regulatory burdens of the dandies.

THE LONELY, YET ALL-KNOWING STRANGER

We've all seen the movies where a dusty lone stranger walks into a saloon, and everyone turns their head to look. The piano player stops, all the poker games cease, and the bartender gives an anxious look, fearful of a gunfight happening right then and there. At that point, the stranger heads to the bar sitting down, and has a drink all alone while everyone watches. I often use this description to inspire people toward the benefits of influence leadership while in the modern professional business world. It describes how it often feels to be the one leading as opposed to the one following. Walking into a board room filled with people who react similarly can be daunting. Still, the perspective of understanding the role of influence leadership is never-the-less every bit as needed as capital or a product to work with.

The world doesn't need, especially in business, more piano players in a saloon, more drinkers, more card players, or prostitutes. There are always plenty of them, and if left to their own devices, maniacal activities will permeate the climate under their rambunctious influence. That is why the lonesome stranger concept is such a popular motif in American Westerns. When there is trouble, the solutions often come from the mysterious outsider or the one who is not spending their time in consumption activities but functioning from a higher order. So when an influence leader enters the room, and everyone goes silent to await what they might do or say, the stage is set for a change, and everyone knows it.

However, to have such an effect, the influence leader must have some exceptional reputation that sets this person apart from the rest of the saloon's inhabitants. There need to be stories of their antics which consist of bravery and color, which sets them apart from everyone otherwise consumed. The nature of influence leadership isn't to be everyone's friend but the person everyone secretly wants to be. The people in the saloon don't, after all, want to whore themselves out to prostitutes. They don't want to be in a drunken situation. They certainly don't want to bet away the last of their dollars in a poker game with a table full of desperados. They want to be that person at the bar who just walked in, making everyone else stop; it is the fantasy of most everyone, even if they do lack the courage on their own to be that person.

And that is the essence of leadership, especially on the influence side of things. If you would like to be such a person, then you must live your life in such a way that sets you apart from the rest of the crowd. You can't just be an influential leader during the eight to ten hours that you might be professionally employed; you need to be one even at two in the A.M., while the rest of the world sleeps. You need to be that person while at the shopping mall or the school band concert you attend to watch your children play. To be an effective influence leader, you always need to be such a person and let the stories of your antics arrive in the ears of the masses unmolested. That is when you will have earned the right to step into a room and have it silenced with your presence as everyone awaits a breath from you.

Knowing that the stories come from individual behavior, which naturally magnifies with each ear that listens to the latest rendition of the tales, you don't have to go out looking for adventures to exploit to unleash your reputation. That will happen on its own; all you need to do is live your life honestly and authentically. Don't be a phony; participate in events, and the stories will form themselves. All you need to focus on is being yourself twenty-four hours a day. Don't try to be other people, just be yourself, and the legend of your life will grow appropriately. That is, after all, why everyone stops when such a person would enter a saloon. Someone out there in the world has done things the rest of them haven't, and that makes the influence leader one of the most sought-out figures in the history of the world—because so few people genuinely live authentically. They are waiting to live through someone else, but they lack the courage to do it themselves.

Of course, what we teach in our education systems, we encourage our students to grow up to become drunks, whores, and piano players reading someone else's sheet music. We teach them to pay for their pleasures when the impulse strikes and that if they can't manage to save enough money to earn it through diligence, then to gamble what they do have in a game of chance, hoping to hit the jackpot so that they can waste it away on pleasure for a brief moment. We don't teach students to think independently and be that lonely figure who enters such a place for some mysterious, otherworldly need, functioning from another motive at the bar sipping on a drink with their back to the room. Yet, that is what it feels like to be a leader. The world wants more than anything to follow a leader. But nobody teaches a leader how to be one.

Every business in the world wants almost more than anything to have such leaders in their organizations. Someone who can walk into a room and get everyone to follow without saying much. Leaders can be good or evil, and people will follow either because it is their nature. However, the business looking to do well needs good people who are good people all day, all days of the week. The more stories of adventure and mayhem that follow, the more of an influence leader they'll become. What makes these people so valuable is that such a reputation cannot be purchased; it must be lived. You can't fake influence leadership. You simply must live a good life and let the adventures of your travels proceed with you. Once you do that, you will have set yourself apart from the crowd, and they will yearn with all their effort to follow. That is why they turn and look when such a person enters the saloon. That is why the music stops, and all attention is paid to the lonely stranger. The first thought is that such an individual is a threat to the natural order of things, but the second is that perhaps there is a person who knows where a great treasure is, so they will follow if there will be profit in it for them. The silence is in all the minds scheming in the room. They want to know how to befriend such a person and get what they can profit for themselves. That is the nature of influence leadership. To have it, the leader can't seek the acceptance of those who would follow. They must be out in front of the social norms of the culture they are entering. And not leave any holes in their persona that might reveal they are otherwise just like everyone else. Nobody wants to follow an average person; they want someone who knows where the treasures are, so silence is always the first reaction to such a person. For the influence leader, that is their greatest weapon.

CHAPTER NOTES:

a. Influence leadership is a lonely endeavor; the world doesn't need more bartenders, drinkers, card players, and prostitutes. Solutions come from those not engaged in those activities.
b. You can't cheat a reputation; the way to become an influence leader is to live that life every hour of the day, all days of the week.
c. Being an influence leader is the person everyone secretly wants to be but is often hated because most don't dare to embrace such a responsibility.
d. We don't teach leadership in our education institutions. Leadership is born from experience; you can't cheat the system to be one.

SPEED DOESN'T COMPROMISE ACCURACY AMONG THE BEST

Many types of shooting sports are very beneficial in honing the mind toward good thinking on matters due to the discipline and diligence it takes to shoot a gun at a target. My choice of Cowboy Fast Draw is in the timed nature of the action instead of more leisurely sports, like golf, where you can take your time to get the correct elements together to perform the task. The pressure of time is needed to get the proper practice to improve human performance. In shooting sports, including SASS (Single Action Shooting Society) and other modern equivalents with updated semi-automatic weapons, time pressure is significant in pushing human limits where they are needed most.

In business, nearly an hour-by-hour mandate requires you to be fast on your feet and decisive. Whether it is a tenuous call with a supplier or customer or a challenge within your organization brought to you via chaos and mayhem, being fast to a resolution is a particular skill. For me, Cowboy Fast Draw is one of the best methods of achieving that needed speed of thought. In many meetings that I've been in when people say that somebody is "shooting from the hip," they mean it as an insult and imply that the action is reckless and inaccurate. Yet in Cowboy Fast Draw, in the modern sense, with the use of wax bullets and electronic strike targets, any shooter can find that being able to draw and hit a target in under half a second is one of the most challenging things a person can do. And once that task is mastered, quick thoughts come in abundance, directly applicable to the business mind.

The assumption of that "shooting from the hip" statement is that the best way to hit a target is to line up the sites toward an objective and perform breathing and hand control rituals to put the bullet where you want it. And of course, this is an excellent way to go about hitting an objective if you have the leisure of unlimited time. However, often we don't have such a condition. Time and pressure are very much part of the shooting experience when simulating a life situation, such as hitting a target faster than the target might react to us. In typical gun duels, the common thought is that the goal would be to get your gun out of the holster first and land a shot on your opposition before they could hit you. Gunfighters like Wild Bill Hickock may not have been the first to fire in a gunfight, but they were the most accurate. So finding that correct balance of speed and accuracy is paramount to such a successful undertaking.

However, accuracy is the most favored approach these days in modern business, whereas speed is nearly ignored. Many people that you will encounter are depressed on Mondays, self-absorbed by Wednesday, and clocked out into weekend activities by Friday. Their minds are not much on their work. Work is tragically viewed as an impediment to happiness, which of course, we are all told is the essential thing in the world these days. Nobody does teach that good work is the key to happiness, and leaving many un-hit targets in the field once a weekend arrives is one of the most stressful things a person can do to themselves. Through procrastination, especially when the work needs to be done, if the work is not connected to the person's innate needs for achieving those tasks, failure always follows.

After a particularly stressful day or week for me, shooting a few hundred shots of gunfire downrange at some target is very satisfying, and it brings all the problems of the world into focus. Shooting sports can be costly, but I never regret spending the money. Cowboy Fast Draw and the use of wax bullets, the cost of shooting is greatly diminished, so at the end of a hard day, or even before starting, you can shoot in the comfort of your own home and achieve much the same diligence. Of course, the first step is in knowing what the target is and in hitting it. In business, it is always important to clearly understand what targets you are trying to hit and to make sure to do so. But the second and most crucial part of Cowboy Fast Draw is hitting that target in less than a second. Learning to think that fast and act accurately under such conditions is a great way to hone the mind toward pressured thinking when it counts and has a more significant percentage of hit targets per attempt. Our life games should reflect the needs of professions, and in business, we don't have all day to make a decision or even a week. Most of the time, decisions need to be made fast, faster than other people can even think, and that is the way to win in these exchanges, thinking faster and more accurately than everyone else.

The people who have started the rumors about "shooting from the hip" have been spreading false statements not to have themselves embarrassed with their tendency toward slow thinking. Learning to shoot and hit targets in milliseconds has a direct impact on thinking under all circumstances. To maintain those skills, the lazy-minded, those who hate Mondays, call Wednesdays "hump days" and look forward to Friday because it means it's the end of the workweek for them, who spread the falsehoods. They didn't want to live up to the expectations that come with such fast and accurate thinkers. When a person trains themselves to think like a gunfighter under matters of pressure and need, every day of the week is an opportunity, and the joys of life aren't in being off the battlefield and away from anxiety, but in being in the middle of it under the most adverse conditions.

Training a mind to think in the healthiest way to deal with stress and pressure is the true path to happiness and success. The fear that most have about life, in general, is that they may not be prepared for whatever may happen, so yes, they do dread Mondays and look forward to Fridays so they can take off their armor and safely live life in a hammock sipping on a drink glad to have lived through the week. But when you think like a gunfighter, who can hit a target in less than half a second, you don't worry about such things. You look forward to each challenge because it's a chance to unleash the skills you have acquired in practice and expand your legendary status among the observers. Even on Saturdays and Sundays, you are thinking correctly about challenges because your mind is in the arena and not in the stands observing. To such a healthy mind, everything is an opportunity. Due to your speed and accuracy under pressure, you know you can handle anything and therefore fear nothing, making you much more effective as a leader and a merchant of dreams to an economy in need of such people.

CHAPTER NOTES:

a. Shooting sports like Cowboy Fast Draw forces participants to increase their concept of speed and accuracy in hitting targets with timed pressure.
b. When saying that someone is "shooting from the hip" it's not an admission of reckless action, but that the competent gun handler is so familiar with the situation that they can achieve speed and accuracy with the gun coming right out of the holster.
c. Lazy people who are not committed to their work like to hide their lack of skill behind a perception that speed equals recklessness.
d. For the good and competent, speed and accuracy are signs of goodness and effectiveness. Such a way of thinking is directly applicable in any business environment.

DRESS TO KILL

There is one undeniable truth that cannot be ignored, the way you dress has a significant impact on the trajectory of your life. If you dress like a ragtag, barely getting along type of person, then your life will reflect that outward appearance. The mind has a unique way of making in reality whatever it is you're thinking. And with that understanding, the global trend to conduct life as a "business casual" dress code is reflected in the generally poor performance of today's industry. The experimental nature of the "tech boom" approach had short-lived gains due to the dynamic character. Still, the movement's sustainability has put too much emphasis on a lackadaisical approach to business interaction that is not conducive to the needs of our time. There was a reason that our older generations wore ties to work every day, and there is a valid argument for returning to that practice, not just in looking nice, but in the way it projects your commitment to whatever you are working on.

Gunfighters who had successfully won duals and had success at the poker table tended to dress up a bit to separate themselves from the dusty range dweller who staggered into town looking for drunkenness and cheap company smelling like they hadn't showered in days and looking like it. The professional gunfighters showed their station more often than not so that everyone knew it before even attempting a conflict that the dressed-up gun wielder had seen success in life and that they might know a thing or two. Their outward appearance indicated that they weren't just the average slugs barely scrapping together two pennies.

People judge; whether that is a correct thing is a pointless question because it's a fact of life. If you show up somewhere looking like an average person rolling out of bed in the morning, people will be looking for leverage against you. They will take notice that you didn't think enough of yourself to do the extra bit of dressing in the morning. Like it or not, how you dress and present yourself will make a big difference in how much success or little you achieve in life. Business is all about opening doors, and once you step in, what you do with that opportunity. So, if you dress poorly, a lot of doors won't even come open. That's not to say that you can't be a complete slob and be successful. Thinking in the way of a gunfighter, a down-dressed appearance might cause an opponent to underestimate you, which could work to an advantage. But common practice dictates that if you are good, you should not seek to trick others into underestimating you. And if you are good, how you dress will naturally filter away all the attempts against you by lower aptitude challengers. Beating those challengers might be easy wins, but they are also a waste of time. It's best to spend your time on the battles that matter.

Respect is precisely why I wear a tie to my professional excursions. It shows respect for the occasions, but there is more to it than that. To me, wearing a tie is like wearing a nicely holstered gun in the time of the gunfighters; it represents an armed professional who is in a league of their own and should be dealt with in that fashion. It also sorts out the riff-raff from the truly competent, not that it is fashionable to make such value judgments, but such is the way of life. Wearing a tie is not a promise that the people showing off such a concern are on the up and up. But to the viewer, the necktie represents competency and leadership. Just as the professional gunfighter would dress with a bit of decoration and nicely polished leather, the necktie is that visual reference from yesteryear, which states here is a professional, proceed with respect.

When four people gather at a meeting, and three of them are dressed business casual, and the last of them is dressed more professionally, the psychological leverage of the meeting will go to the person wearing a tie. It is the business attire for a woman in various styles beyond jeans and a casual top. Dressing down for such occasions indicates that the participants are nonchalant about the business and do not care about the outcome. This may or not be accurate, but the dress certainly indicates that sentiment. However, when a tie is presented, it is similar to the professional gunfighter there with their finely polished boots, impeccable vest, and shirt with a pocket watch laced across their midsection. A hat without bullet holes or has had the color robbed of it from days on the open range beaten to death by an unforgiving sun and torrential downpours. Dressing well is defiance against nature and the elements it throws at us as a civilization. The well-dressed gunfighter turned businessperson states with their power dress above those elements and are masters of competency. Only a successful person could even afford to look that way when the frontier living conditions worked against it with every hour of the day. Dressing well is a defiance of how things are or have always been. This respect for the conditions of market exchange is why aristocratic society emphasized such a thing and why modern politicians do the same. In many ways, they have given the practice a bad name. The trend toward casual was to say to the world that the wearer wasn't a phony.

Yet as stated, the wrong name given to formal dress was in the phonies of the world trying to appear as they were not, so their use of the strategy was insincere. It doesn't take much to test them and discover that their brains are often empty, and they hope that their dress keeps challengers away from discovering their secret. The method worked because dressing well is an innate understanding among all people. The well-dressed person has come into resources above and beyond most people's station, and whether or not they are phonies or deadly gunfighters from the past who are highly competent, it is better to dress up than to dress down.

The main issue is respect; even if you are coming to an occasion to kill, you can respect the participants, which is the game's name. That is also why dressing well gives leverage in a situation where everyone else is unprepared. At the primal level, we all understand the game, whether the rules are discussed openly. As people, we know how things work, dressing well, separating ourselves from others, and always help secure whatever position we may be representing. When they say "dressed to kill," this is where the utterances come from. And every morning when you get up, you should be thinking this way. Because as all professional gunfighters know from the days passed, any advantage you can get is a good thing and dramatically increases your success ratio. So use everything you have and make it so in your mind, even in the things that people don't see. Because in your mind, you know, and when the bullets start flying, that is ultimately the difference between winning and losing.

CHAPTER NOTES:

a. The way you dress has a significant impact on the direction of your life. The mind has a unique way of bringing about what it thinks about, starting with presenting yourself to the world.
b. Gunfighters who dressed well did so to separate themselves from losers to reduce the risks that might come their way otherwise. People may attack if they think you are an easy target.
c. Business is all about opening doors. If you dress like a slob, many of those doors will never come open.
d. Dressing well shows respect for the occasion. Dressing down shows a lack of commitment to the events of our day.

THE PROFICIENCY OF SIX-SHOOTEROLOGY

There is a common falsehood in business, speed and accuracy do not go together in life. You can only have one and not the other. When the pressure is intense, the thought process goes as such; we should all slow things down to get our bearings on the situation and then resume our activities toward a resolution through calmness and clarity. Thinking of the cultures who had migrated into North America during Western Expansion, the trending thought at the time would have been to smoke a pipe and think about the problem, perhaps even pray to some bird in bringing divine assistance to the matter. Yet, that is not the way the West was won as the term often phrases it. More often than not, speed is needed to resolve a matter, and accuracy is demanded because you won't get a second swipe.

In shooting sports such as Cowboy Fast Draw, you must feel your target; you don't have time to aim. Through lots of practice and diligence, you pull the trigger before any thought of lining up a site along your barrel toward a target can be thought about. You must draw and shoot almost as fast as a person blinks an eye, which is around .115 of a second. We are shooting in Cowboy Fast Draw around .350 to .420, so we are talking about breakneck speeds, and we are expected to hit our targets at various distances. When practicing this sport, I never think about aiming; there isn't time for it, even though it's an essential part of the activity. You must trust that you will hit your target as a natural byproduct of the work you have done through all your practice and that the main thing to react to is the speed at which you act.

Like any great athlete who can throw a baseball off their back foot deep from the shortstop position to a long arch to the first basemen just before a runner hits the base, the skill is in the unconscious understanding, not the precision of knowledge. The infielder gets the throw accurately without thinking about it because they have practiced so much and have become so skilled that the conditions of competition give the ball no choice but to arrive at the target correctly. The modern shooters of timed sports have shot so many times that the muscle memory of their hands, arms, and shoulders knows precisely where they need to be under tenuous conditions. Accuracy is determined, therefore, by diligence, practice, and preparation. Taking your time is not the way to accuracy; it's in knowing what you are doing. Speed, therefore, is in your reaction time to the events of the world around you.

If you are overthinking about hitting your target, you will likely miss under pressure because the mind brings about what it thinks about, and if it is thinking about missing, or avoiding a miss, then that concern will eat up all your success. Before shooting, you must trust that all your hours of practice will result in a hit, leaving your mind free to react to the circumstances, which are the variables of concern.

This applies to business because the pressure is part of good conduct in commerce, and speed and accuracy are very much a part of it. Such art has been somewhat lost to our modern times because the institutional thinking of our day has returned to the native praying over a fire toward the bird gods hoping for supernatural aid rather than relying on skill and perseverance to dominate the day's problems. Superstition has generated falsehoods about how success resides in reality and has permeated our lives primarily unmolested.

For most, work is to be avoided at all costs these days, so practicing our skills is a lost art. Perhaps the work is in reviewing spreadsheets and PowerPoints on a Saturday and Sunday morning before anybody is up in the world to gain practice for when you need to recite those elements to a gathering later in the week. Or maybe it's in catching up with all the emails that you haven't had time for during a busy week so that you can know their contents for the many business calls that will hit you on Monday morning. Doing the extra work when everyone else is sleeping and watching television is the key to acting fast and accurately when demands arrive for a committed approach. The best of the gunfighters who lived through many challenges had a tendency not to consider what might happen if they were hit with a deadly bullet or how they might divert the situation to some other outcome; they simply focused on shooting down their challenger. Their training allowed for an almost unconscious reaction to the shooting mechanisms. The cocking of the gun as it leaves the holster, the leveling of the sites toward the target even as the weapon was next to their hip, these are the ways to perfection. Then the pulling of the trigger before the challenger could even think to blink. That is the way to win in all encounters, and the way to get there is through practice and a 24 hour per day approach to the work involved in knowing what to do precisely when you need to know it.

It's not that people functioning like this are leaving fate to chance. Still, instead, they have developed an ability to control change by controlling destiny, not micromanaging their thoughts, and trusting themselves to do the right thing at just the right time so that they only need to focus on time. Great orators have in common that they trust that their minds will produce the words they need when they need them when speaking. The stumbling around that happens when amateurs talk is that they try to find the words rather than knowing they are already there. Their brains will produce just the correct sequence on a moment's need. Trust in oneself is particularly true of the businessperson who is conversing with someone or many company representatives. Things aren't going well, where it is desperately needed to ease the matter back toward productive discussion. If the businessperson has done their homework and knows the elements of the case in great detail, the words will come. Suppose the businessperson spent their weekend picking flowers and watching gossip on television. In that case, they should not be surprised that they are unprepared when action is needed, and their mind isn't able to produce results because their mind was not on their work, but on everything but.

We are amazed by displays in sports of speed and accuracy where the athlete performs wonderfully under pressure. But what we often don't see are the many thousands of hours of practice it took to get into that form. And such a concept is no different for the shooter under timed conditions. It's not a miracle that shooters can shoot so extremely fast. It comes with the excellent practice that is involved in becoming that good. Then to consider that when a mind is accustomed to thinking so quickly about a sport they are in, then the same methods can be beneficial in their role in business. Suppose leisure time is spent thinking swiftly, then in the professional part of a business where quick wit and solid decision-making under tremendous pressure are demanded. In that case, the mind is already in that realm, and the businessperson will be much more effective. Such people will be heads and shoulders better than their rivals who have not arrived thus prepared.

CHAPTER NOTES:

a. The perception about speed and accuracy is that you can only have one or the other. This is incorrect. We should master both to be the most effective.
b. Speed is often needed to resolve a matter. If you take too long to aim at anything, you will likely lose the chance at success.
c. Speed is acquired in the unconscious understanding of the process from the vigorous practice and trust in your abilities. Those who say they need more time are unskilled in the arts of speed.
d. Claiming speed is not achievable or reckless are those too lazy to develop the skill of speed. These days it's a lost art to gain skills all days of the week, all hours of the day. Skill is built best when gained when others are sleeping and resting. Those are the times to become better than the competition.

DON'T LOOK BACK AT THE POSSE

One thing is for sure wherever human beings gather, especially in places of business, one of the most significant concerns that spring forth is whether or not they have the approval of their peers. Most people spend enormous amounts of their life concerned about peer approval, and of course, this is a mechanism of control that some utilize over others. When consent is sought but is regulated by others, the power goes to those who issue out that approval. Thus, it is the means of control that most dominates most human activity. Until the invention of the gunfighter came along, which made the opinions of others a much more secondary concern. The nature of frontier life and its loneliness conditioned the minds of a few to live without such needs, and the guns they wore made a compulsion to action an impossibility. If one person pushed another too much, a gunfight was more likely to emerge rather than a strongly worded complaint to human resources.

Freedom from peer approval was fertile ground for developing a new kind of leader in the world. The idea of an armed individual who didn't have to be compelled into some action without their full endorsement was quite a stepping stone of human achievement. History had otherwise mandated yielding to the opinions of others, or else. If they were good with their aim and fast enough on the draw, the gunfighter could feel confident that most of the people they were dealing with in the world could not beat them. There was a new kind of freedom in that understanding that resides in all American society's core values. Naturally, this same psychological transition flows over into the business world and everywhere humans gather for communication and imaginative endeavors.

Only in the modern world, guns may not be needed to have such a position of independence. The contemporary leader functions in much the same way as the traditional gunfighter assured in their roles. Typically, they do not look over their backs at every minor threat out there because they are more intelligent, faster, and more competent to deal with those threats than anybody else around. When you work hard to be better than the average, there is no need to look around at who might be scratching at your heels, hoping that some tragedy will befall you so that they might advance in life.

After all, that is the motive behind most gossip. To poke and probe until some weakness is found in whoever is considered out in front of everyone else. Once that weakness is found, peers hope to exploit it to have a chance to be at the top of the food chain. Only what they forget to consider is that the best gets that way through hard work and in honing their skills. They don't arrive there with gossip. What is built in such a way falls apart just as fast. People made into power on the coattails of gossip and hearsay are quick to lose in the same way. Those who are good at what they do need not look over their backs at those clawing at them. They just need to continue to be the best, and everything else will take care of itself.

It may seem unfair that just by doing good, so many targets are placed around the necks of the competent that the people who work hardest to be the best they can be are even shot at in the first place by so many jealous boot lickers. But never forget that the cheaters and the lazy made the rules of the world, so to make things easier for themselves, not to serve justice. If a reasonable person stumbles, the world will report it, but if a loser falls flat on their face and people walk over them without noticing, it should not be a surprise. That is the way of the world, and fairness has nothing to do with it. Just accept that if you want to be good, the world will want to tear away at you because they don't want the expectations that come with that effort. They will want to destroy you so that they don't have to fear you always outmatching them in everything they haphazardly attempt to do.

By coming to terms with that nature of the human spirit, new freedom comes to the mind of what traditionally was the gunfighter, the one armed and ready for anything. Under no circumstances should a great person be concerned about the feeble attempts by others to tear away at their reputations; deeds speak for themselves. Winners don't need to look behind them; only losers do. Losers are always the ones looking at who is in front of them. Winners are out in front and keep their eyes on the prize. This approach is best for the gunfighter, except when the potential for being shot in the back looms. Even so, the best gunfighter will know and can defend themselves when needed just through the nature of being the fastest to react.

Such is the scenario in countless Westerns. The gunfighter steps into a saloon sitting at the bar with their back to the room, their hat pulled down. Their concealed face inviting challengers to make their move. When you are the best, everyone else is at a disadvantage because, like the proper strategic high ground of any military endeavor being the most sought-after position in a conflict, a reputation serves just as well. The weak always must worry about overcoming the strong; the best is the best for a reason. And those who become so often are not gifted with that reputation; they earn it, win by win. Once you've won enough, you can sit with your back to the room and can feel when some evil character is about to take a shot. In that way, you control their actions by determining when and where they will attempt. Your back to them is just another method of control, so use it to a significant effect. But not before your reputation is so that others become used to looking at your back for a long time.

CHAPTER NOTES:

a. Most people waste most of their life worrying about the approval of their peers. That gives away power to everyone but you.
b. Freedom from approval is the vacuum where leadership is born and was developed naturally in the American gunfighter.
c. If you are better, faster, and more intelligent than the competition, you do not need to look over your back at those hoping you fail so they can overcome you. Make it so that you always stay in front of them, robbing them of their dreams.
d. The cheaters and looters have made the rules of the world, hoping it will give them a chance to take over the best without having to do the work. Yet when you are the best, everyone else is at a disadvantage. Keep it that way.

BOOTLICKERS ARE WHAT THEY EAT

Just as we say that a good gunfighter should not look back over their shoulder at their competition clawing at their heels, neither should they do any bootlicking to those considered ahead of them socially on the pecking order of societal hierarchy. Most of us working in the business are not running the companies moving and shaking the world, or we don't own those companies. Usually, the work is done on behalf of those who hire us. However, unlike the bounty hunters, when we are hired, we are meant to help change the culture for the better, so our talent acquisition is more permanent than just solving a short-term quarterly problem. Ideas like this can be murky, so the concept of a lone gunfighter riding into a town that requires their services acts as a proper narrative for understanding this largely misunderstood concept about how the world works. Bootlicking is not the way to rise to the top.

A gunfighter looking for work sees that the town has a sheriff, a mayor, several prominent businesspeople, yet they have problems with crime. Bandits are running the saloon by sheer force. Cattle rustlers hang out on the edge of town trying to enact taxes on goods coming in and out of the settlement, and among the many prominent members of the community, corruption has seeped in. The criminal element pays too well, so the temptation is all too consuming. What the town needs are someone to take on these losers and restore justice. It does not need another boot licker hanging out around the sheriff or mayor trying to brown-nose their way into a good job. The gunfighter needs to let everyone know that they are available, and the people who need the services will seek them out. There is no need for kiss assing.

Ass kissing, of course, runs counter to everything most of us have been taught about the way the world works. Most of us assume that jobs and positions are handed out to people who favor those in power, not that those in power will admit that they need something we have to offer. In the same mindset that the gunfighter should not worry about who is always trying to beat them in life, the focus should always be on being the best at whatever one is doing. The concern of one's time should never be to "fake it until you make it," as the term goes. Gaining favor with the powerful is not the way to become powerful. And getting a vital job just because you managed to make someone like you defeats the purpose of doing such a job. When a job needs to be done, such as the illustrative example of running bad guys out of a saloon or ruining a cattle rustling network, a great and competent gunfighter is needed for the job, not another boot licking loser for which the world is already filled.

While it's true that much of the world promotes in the fashion of favorability, this is always why most things fail, because the right people are not in the correct positions to solve the problems as they occur. Bootlicking does not make for a better anything; it only hides the actual needs of the most viable candidates. People in leadership positions who insist on promoting bootlickers are destined to fail, so no honorable person should ever seek a job with such people. That is why it is essential to view your role as a gunfighter coming into a town in need of their services, and simply letting their skills do all the talking is the best approach. Forget about the fancy dinners and the drinks or join that social club that the mayor has going on. Just do what you do and let the good deeds be your resume.

The network game of its "whom you know, not what you know" was a falsehood created by the lazy and disreputable to advertise their own con game to the world. Because what happens is that someone gets the important job of running the bad guys out of the saloon; they aren't very skilled. They obtained the job because they curried favor with the mayor's wife, and she put in a good word, or the sheriff liked that the gunfighter tipped their hat when walking by. Now, a situation needs real skill and action, yet the new hire doesn't know what to do, so they write letters, put up signs, and try every passive-aggressive trick in the book to alter the situation. Which, of course, the bandits will only laugh. That essentially is the state of our present world in most cases, especially in business. What is needed is the gunfighter who can read the strongest and fastest from the slowest and dumbest. To go into that saloon and clean house without even breaking a sweat. Fancy talk and pandering tactics will not work with such people, only superior skill and resolve. When the town lacks such characteristics, and the gunfighter has them naturally, no bootlicking will solve it. Only exceptional talent will.

Once the threats are contained, those in power will find the gunfighter a danger. The gunfighter will have to watch for the many poisons sent their way to eliminate their threat to that power. But understand that those who obtain power through bootlicking expect to maintain that order, and once it is threatened, they will collapse on themselves looking over their shoulders at you. All you need to be is the best, and the rest will work itself out. They will pay you to stay around because they are incompetent and can't solve problems independently. And just by being around, they will destroy themselves, worrying about you taking their power away from them. If you can keep away from their poisons, they will have no choice but to start honoring you just out of their own needs for self-preservation.

Bootlicking and ass-kissing should have never been a part of how we do business in any fashion. Only respect and honor should be applicable, recognizing the most skilled jobs that require those services. Yet, the lazy and corrupt have had their hand in the business of making laws and social policy for a long time. They rationalized that they could not compete in the world honestly, so they turned instead to the social networks to protect them from harsh work and insulate themselves from the reality of competency. To maintain that need, they need competent people around them, so if you think like a gunfighter who is the best around, there will always be a need for you in a job and paying what you're worth. The people who suck up and bootlick do so because they have no other skills to offer but to polish the egos of those with already damaged reputations. That is not only the way to failure but is the basic foundation of all corruption, and any good, honorable gunfighter wouldn't be happy with such an arrangement. And that certainly isn't the way to truly get rich in this world. The best and most successful way to a good life is to have a skill nobody else has and use it where needed most. In the world of the gunfighter, that was always the case because few dared to face down evil when it appeared. But of course, evil presents itself in many different forms all the time, even sometimes as angels. Bootlickers don't know the difference.

CHAPTER NOTES:

a. To improve your life, you should do the work at becoming the best, not taking the easy path of boot-licking people you think are above you in life.
b. Gaining favor with the powerful is not the way to become powerful. The lack of skill once you've acquired a powerful position, you will be discovered as a phony.
c. Gunfighters need to know the strongest and fastest, from the slowest to the dumbest. Only exceptional talent can understand how to sort through this process. Boot-licking only hides the incompetent from judgment.
d. Social networks are designed to protect the worthless from the competency needed for reality. Bootlickers have no other skills but to appease those superior to them.

EVERYONE ISN'T IMPORTANT

This is one of the hardest things for many, to value your own time and distribute it correctly among the many others you deal with. And the higher up the food chain of importance you become, the more this will be a problem. You don't have time to deal with everyone, not to let them consume your time on things that are not important to your task. Even so, you cannot allow your predilection toward human acceptance to drive you to waste time on other people's trivial pursuits. As much as you might like to, there just isn't time for it. When you become the top of a company and hold the keys to many other people's success, and they perceive, due to their training and life experiences, that the way to advance in life is to brown-nose you, you cannot further harm them by endorsing their vision. They need to know that the only way to your heart is through doing a good job. Your time is valuable and cannot be distributed uselessly among those who seek leverage through false friendships.

The gunfighter has removed all the criminal elements from a town, the sheriff is happy, the mayor is also. The merchants are appreciative and find themselves giving the gunfighter free clothes, free food, and access to the saloon to keep the prospect of more menaces only in the imaginations of the criminal. Due to the excellent work of the gunfighter, the town is happy with the heroics, and all is well. Except that everywhere the gunfighter goes, someone is there looking to talk their ear off. One lady wants to talk about the weather in the street; another man desires to speak to the gunfighter about farming and the challenges of this year's harvest. The sheriff wants to tell stories about their youth. The mayor all their social connections waiting for the gunfighter to perk up at one of them, which might be dangled later for leverage in the way politicians think. The gunfighter may like all these people and want to do well by them. Still, all that noise is very distracting to the businesses of sorting out evil and using the skills of speed and diligence to put down threats to the order before they even appear ghost-like on the horizon.

In a typically busy day for the successful person, hundreds, if not thousands of people to interact with, you may only have a few seconds to deal with those most critical to your tasks. There are phone calls to return, emails to answer. Of course, there are meetings, lots of them. And the more you've worked up the ladder of importance, the more sessions that you'll have to attend. These days it's not unusual to have conversations with people over a 24-hour day in three to four time zones, and those are meetings on top of the other meetings you need to attend within your organization. While following all these events and conducting all this effort, you will pass people, and each of them would like some of your time. Of course, even if you could, there would be no way to spend time with all of them and give them 5 to 10 minutes of your day because you don't have it, especially if you are successful. Being successful and staying that way requires you to do what you do that is unique to the world, and if you are wasting time on trivial nonsense, you obviously won't be doing your best work which put you in such need, to begin with.

This is why shooting sports involving speed and accuracy can help with social requirements. By learning to target the correct things to shoot at through practice, the gunfighter knows that they don't have all day to aim at a target. They must pull the trigger properly to be successful, and the same rules apply to other people. Interacting with others requires a concise approach; you don't have all day. But people being people also need to be nurtured as an aspect of leadership. That is why your mind must be fast, respectful, but not allowed to linger on trivial nonsense and doubts. You may speak with someone politely but know that you don't have much time to hear about their cat, or their insurance policies, or to complain about their spouse. Give them a targeted amount of time out of politeness but move to the next target quickly so that you can keep your mind on your tasks and continue doing what made you successful, to begin with.

The gunfighter in the town needs to stay sharp and keep in the frame of mind that dispersed the outlaws. Luxurious thinking will distract the mind from the task at hand, so the successful gunfighter would not accept such impediments. A simple nod of acknowledgment or even just a smile is all that is needed to let others know that you see and hear them. But also that there is no open door to enter into the mind of the gunfighter. A business today is filled with many more distractions; a polite acknowledgment of others is all that needs to be applied. A successful person like the gunfighter was made that way by doing what they do best. They don't need to waste time on small talk and gossip because targets to hit and time is not on anybody's side. All the talk from others is only a distraction from the objectives. There is very little that anybody will bring to a beneficial conversation, so it is best to avoid those exchanges.

The weak and insecure-minded out there will think that they might learn something important from small talk and gossip, but that isn't success talking; it's the thinking that ruins the world. Going out for a few drinks after work might be viewed as a networking experience and a friendly team-building event. Still, the truth of the matter is that if you keep your mind on your targets, networking is worthless because if you are successful, you will have more people seeking your time than you will ever want to have. Networking turns out to be a big waste of time because once people see that you have something they want to be associated with, you will have more friends and network partners than you will ever have time to deal with in a thousand lifetimes. So don't waste time on nonsense and innuendo. Keep your mind on your targets, and don't allow others to distract you from your objectives because the danger is always looming around the corner, and you won't want to miss it when it arrives.

CHAPTER NOTES:

a. The higher up the food chain you become, the more people will seek your attention with attempts at boot-licking. You cannot be pulled into every little detail of people's lives and still do your job of management.
b. If you are dealing with hundreds of people per day and they all want 5 minutes of your time, you will find that you must sort out the trivial nonsense for your preservation. Being respectful to the people without wasting time on minor issues is one of the key reasons you must think fast and accurately to determine essential information from nonessential information.
c. If you are successful, there will be more people seeking your time than you will ever have time to deal with, don't waste time networking with drinks after work because there won't be time for it.
d. It is hard for many people to value their time enough to make determinations on its dispersal since out of compassion, you want to make everyone happy. But not at the expense of your objective.

WINNING

For several reasons, the word "winning" has taken on a negative connotation. Terms like "it doesn't matter if you win or lose, it's how you play the game" are complete nonsense, perhaps one of the dumbest things anybody has ever said. Winning is the goal of everything, especially in business. It sets the bar others will have to follow. The more you win, the better those around you will naturally be because competition will be improved by the bar you raised, resulting in greater expectations going forward. When you win, you have achieved something, and the results are excellent output. While it's true you may not always win, the trick in life is to win more than you lose, constantly pushing yourself to a more significant percentage of victory. The wins are better if your competition is good because the quality of the success is much improved.

For the gunfighter, winning was a necessity. There wasn't a second place. That is essentially why the gunfighting motif has permeated American society so valiantly over the years. The close association with winning and gunfighting has turned the whole concept into romantic notions that have stayed in our imaginations. And for a good reason. Everything you approach in life, you should expect to win. If you don't, then you need to figure out why and get better. But to get into that winning mindset, practicing gunfighting is an excellent way to think because, in practice, there was always a finality to it if you did lose a match.

The celebrity many gunfighters enjoyed who had survived many confrontations was justified because the odds of winning more than once was not in their favor. Turning the odds against oneself into a positive ratio is something that deserves some level of honor because it's such a hard thing to do. When everyone is out for a win, getting a more significant percentage in your favor is an ominous enterprise. Wins are always honorable, such as the great fight between Edison and Tesla, for which Edison won. The better idea or concept doesn't always win; it's usually the one who thinks they can or expects who does. Wins and losses have lasting impacts on all our futures and should be pursued with zeal due to their implications.

Even great gunfighters ended up losing when their backs were turned or were inebriated with intoxicants once they had let their guard down for one reason or another. These are not tragedies as much as they are life lessons; the goal of all human beings is to win and win at all costs. Once this is understood and embraced, we can all have a much more honest exchange about the nature of existence. The best kind of world is one where winning and losing are assumed, not avoided because the byproduct of the competition is a life improvement, which ends up being suitable for everyone.

When competitors shake hands at the end of a match, the loser shouldn't go off stomping in retaliation, acting as if they will never get a chance to win again. They should honor the person who won even if their feelings are hurt because the win conditions improved. The level of competition drives such urges, and the by-product is always an improvement over the previous state. In modern Cowboy Fast Draw, without the level of competition present, the times that are now achieved likely wouldn't have taken place, which sometimes pushes into the .200s of a second. If everyone just practiced in their garage, probably the times would stay in the .400s. Still, for the chance to win a trophy and to be called the best, even if just for that day, human beings will push themselves incredibly to achieve what others thought impossible. The joy of winning has uncovered many traits of human achievement that wouldn't have been unleashed otherwise, so winning has a lot more to do with our culture than many would otherwise attribute.

There are opportunities to win every day in business, whether in the sales objectives, a new contract, or turning an angry supplier or customer into an ally; the business world is every bit as competitive and deadly as gunfighting in the previous century. A loss in a gunfight might lead to the death of the loser. A failure in a business exchange might end a career or a reputation. Many people losing a reputation for winning are just as bad as death because it can be hard to build up over time. A loss of reputation can leave such a person not wanting to continue playing the great games with as many chips going into the pot; they may want to play it safe to protect their victorious reputation. But as we know, often, that is how one loses in life; playing not to lose becomes subtly playing not to win. The games of our leisure certainly do flow over into the games of real life. Once a person loses that edge to continue winning, they start losing more often. In business, that is how a previously great person becomes a failure "has been" because they stop yearning to win due to age or simply losing competitive spirit.

With that understood, it is not harmful to want to win. It is very healthy and needed. People who succeed tend to dress better and like to show off their gains acquired materially because, like a trophy, it is evidence that they have been winning. Businesspeople who go to lunch or dinner with other businesspeople have a good reason to judge the kind of car their opponent drives. How they dress, what their spouse looks like because all those indicators reveal if that person has won more than they have lost in life, and will have a lot to do with how the current business transaction will go. It isn't harmful to go out and get that sports car to let others know that you have won enough in life to earn one. Like the gunfighter who dresses up a bit to reveal they have become wealthy with their guns, the modern businessperson could and should do the same to let their competition know that winning will not be easy. It may even get into their heads that a challenge may not be in their best interest, and they'll give up in their minds before the competition even starts. Regardless of the case, the concept of winning should be embraced and encouraged because if there is any real tangible meaning in life, it is to yearn to achieve where others fall short, to win at what we compete in. Even if winning doesn't happen every time, it should be the goal of everyone because the game of trying to win elevates life for all the participants. The sweetness of victory is something everyone can experience if they play games enough and get used to the pressure. And that sweetness is there for a reason, be it from God or some other element; we are built as humans to win. The more we put ourselves in a position to win, the better. For the gunfighter, winning was a necessity. For the modern businessperson, it is no less critical.

Unlike the finality of a bullet, however, there is a new day for victory in business in most cases. But every occasion should be treated as if it were the last thing you would ever do because the competition of the fantastic games is what matters in the end. It's not so much who gets the trophy, but what is created due to the competition.

CHAPTER NOTES:

a. The term "it doesn't matter if you win or lose, it's how you play the game" is one of the dumbest things ever said by anybody.
b. The trick of the game is always to win more than you lose. And you always want quality wins because they give the endeavor more value.
c. Turning the odds in your favor when winning looks bleak is how to build a much-needed reputation. Look to win at everything and to win at all costs. Even if you don't win, do everything you can to do so. If not, get back at it quickly.
d. The need to push for a win drives innovation beyond what others thought previously impossible. Playing not to lose, however, is the same as playing not to win.

THE CRAFT OF RELOADING

One of the best features of any sport, especially shooting sports, is the maintenance of the gear. Cowboy Fast Draw is particularly the case due to the constant cleaning that has to go on to keep your guns in top shape. To get good at Cowboy Fast Draw, you will have to shoot thousands of rounds in practice, and this too is one of the great benefits, each of those rounds will need to be reloaded by hand. While this can be time-consuming, it is also very therapeutic. The care of weapons, in general, is very conducive for business as the skills applied in that leisure activity directly improve the professional realm due to the focus on individual enjoyment.

One of the great attributes of guns, precisely, is that as they were invented and seeped into our global culture that the governments of more independence for individuals became more popularized. Along with that gain of individually based self-government came more emphasis on individual-based living and, consequently, expanding individually based economies. Options catered to individual tastes instead of villages and cities but for each household. As economic development flowed into that direction where any individual anywhere could have a different pair of pants, a different car, and a different house than their peers, the need for more individual input from businesspeople became much more needed to enter those markets. In most business transactions, especially at a high level, the popular term is to talk about teams of people. Still, in the end, it usually comes down to one individual strategy here and there, which unlocks the potential for all economic expansion.

Standing at a workbench reloading the wax ammunition that goes into Cowboy Fast Draw is a great way to re-center the thoughts of an otherwise fragmented day. Cleaning the guns, the shells, and ultimately putting in new primers and wax bullets into the used cases of Cowboy Fast Draw is a solitary experience that keeps the basics of the whole sport in keen focus. The practice is a constant reminder of the notion that shooting sports, in general, are systematically individually based. If you don't do the work, nobody else will, and if you are not prepared to clean all your equipment, you won't be ready when you need it.

It is easy to feel disjointed and out of focus as the microcosm of events as a businessperson erodes your sense at the end of just about any busy day. For many, there just aren't enough good stress management tools available to such people to properly keep their minds and bodies healthy. It's no accident that many business people suffer from stress-related illnesses, from overeating to heart disease. Stress management is very much part of the job, and managing that stress one of the most significant challenges. After all, what good is that big deal you are closing, which you worked so hard on if you fall over dead from work?

Golf and other sports are good releases of tension. Still, they often involve other people and distract the individual mind tasked to solve whatever problems evolve out of business necessities. That usually leaves the businessperson feeling empty and psychologically depleted, and poor health follows in a predictable pattern. However, with shooting sports, the smell of gunpowder on your fingertips and the satisfaction of performing a crafting activity for personal enjoyment go a long way to re-centering thoughts properly when stress is pounding away at you. Fifteen minutes to half an hour at a workbench working on guns for accurate and fast shooting puts a mind in the right place to solve complicated problems without suffering the crippling effects of stress. If I had to say it, the reloading of Cowboy Fast Draw ammunition and the cleaning of the guns is probably the best aspect of taking up the sport for the person suffering from incredible stress and in need of management.

Once, however, stress has been successfully managed, the mind is good to resume the rigors of daily life. The businessperson will find they are functioning at a much higher capacity for the rigors of life than before. The primal conduct of the mind knowing that what it is practicing is for the good of the individual for which the mind resides motivates it to handle everything better. Once the mind knows the body is working to help it achieve greatness, the withering effects of life have a way of subsiding. Mastery over the elements of chaos percolates into a successful life over everything, from rushing the kids off to soccer practice after a busy day at the office to dealing with several family tragedies, all the while responsible for millions of dollars in sales for that week.

Pressure can be detrimental if not dealt with correctly, and it is under pressure that most of the great things in life come forth. The businessperson should never avoid stress; they should seek out how a tired person seeks a pillow, but for the reverse effects, to be more alive and vibrant than ever. But to endure the pressures of daily life in the world of business, a body and mind must withstand the forces acting against it. For that, some focused time at the workbench with your guns and ammunition is just the right thing. Guns, in general, are very therapeutic; they were invented to usher in the personal defense of one's life. Cleaning and oiling them is a good reminder of what they do for the individual mind in need of some upkeep after a rough day. But the extra element of Cowboy Fast Draw goes even further in allowing you to use those guns more often due to the nature and cost of the wax bullets. It will enable the businessperson to shoot many tens of thousands of shots for the price that would otherwise be prohibitive with standard lead ammunition.

If the samurai warriors trained with wooden swords to hone their skills, the modern gunslingers have wax bullets. And the maintenance of those items does more than keeping the equipment in tip-top condition; it has a tremendous psychological impact on elevated stress from the businessperson's mind, making them ultimately much more effective in a shorter recovery period. After all, that is why we do these kinds of things as humans, to make ourselves happy and to get back on the battlefield as quickly as possible. If that isn't the meaning of life, then what is? We were all born to be in the arena. Even in our leisure, we think about the great battles in front of us and prepare for them. What is a better thing to do in life? It's not that you are thinking of aggression on other people when performing these tasks; the functions themselves reassure the mind that you are caring for its independence of thought, and many of the pressures that had been crushing you will float away by default. You will find yourself a much more effective businessperson, and a better person in general, and a whole lot happier.

CHAPTER NOTES:

a. The maintenance of the gear keeps a mind on the act of the shooting competition. Just as the care of business tools does the same for the industry.
b. Reloading gun ammunition is an excellent way to sort through the fragmented aspects of a busy day. Working out those fragmented thoughts is a good way to manage stress.
c. The businessperson can function at a much higher capacity in life once mastery over stress is introduced.
d. A businessperson should never avoid stress; they should seek it out like a sleepy person seeks a pillow. Use a mechanism for dealing with the pressure to manage the condition, so extra mental capacity is always available for the needs of the business.

YOU HAVE TO PLACE YOUR BETS

As much as it should be cautioned while playing poker that you wait for the right cards to come up, at some point in the game, you will have to push up your bets and place your chips in the middle of the table. A poker game can go on for a long time if the players protect their winnings after each round. The downside to being cautious is that the pot never increases and that nobody at the table ends up being a big winner. So the nature of the game is to push up the pot and get rich, winning the game. Protecting your investments is not a game-winning strategy; it is only a strategy to keep you in the game until you get the right cards, and when you do get them, you must play them correctly.

Many people in life, especially in business, spend most of their experience folding at the end of every hand. Slowly they get some little winnings here and there, and people tell them how smart they are to hold onto their money, and when they come to the end of it, sure they have their pile of protected money, but not much else. Playing it safe leads to a dull life and few opportunities for life-changing wealth. Poker is not a game for such people, the name of the entire thing is to bet and come away with other people's money due to raw nerve and emotional leverage. When your cards come up that you know usually will win a hand, you need to push up the bets. Sometimes you will lose as the other guy might have a better hand, but you must put the doubt in his head that he has the best cards and tempt him to fold. And to play like that, you can't play it safe.

In business, we are tempted by such fates every day. It is easy to fold after every hand, and most of the people you will deal with every day have been taught to do so. Once they learn they are playing with house money, they perceive that the house will want them to protect that investment by folding every round until everyone gets bored and gets up from the table or some miracle happens. They win under no strategic circumstances whatsoever. They might win under those conditions, yet they have no idea why. If they fold after every round, only playing the minimum bets, the pot is very little and only gains back what they have bet over the previous rounds when they happen to win. Then they wonder why they fail in life.

At some point, whether the game is poker or the game is business, you must bet your chips and stand by your cards. Of course, there is a risk; that is the difference between losers and winners; winners can deal with the risk, losers cave to it. The mind of the gunfighter is used to leverage their skill against other's timidity; the trouble is a part of their life. They don't have time to think of whether their skills will be sufficient for the task. They must trust their cards and put their bets on the table at the right moments. They don't want to be reckless over every hand but to be systematic and diligent. When the conditions are right, the chips are pushed into the center of the table for fate's temptations. When doing this, you should always expect to win, even if you are bluffing.

Gun battles and dueling in the early formation of America was a messy business but a necessary one. In many ways, the games of our modern age have replaced that dueling necessity, but the risks are still there. Casinos continue to be a constant source of past time in American life due to the hopeful nature that vast riches can be acquired by playing at the chance. Sometimes it does, but most of the time, winnings are gained by playing highs against lows. Not everyone has the skill to know the difference, just as early gunfighters often didn't live very long when they were reckless with their guns and challenged everyone to everything all the time. Just like in poker, that is an excellent way to go broke. Yet, the need to push the limits is ever-present in American life, and those who don't do so or have some mechanism find themselves bored with life.

Every great hitter in baseball debates about hitting that low sinker down and in; if they miss, they'll look foolish in front of thousands of people, and history will remember it through television. If they make contact, it could be a home run. An excellent stock car racer debates about taking on another driver in the last five laps of the race on the outside to go for a win; if they sit in their number 7 to 15 position and never make a move, they will always be in the middle of the pack. Like the rest of the world, that is how people get stuck in the middle, never great. A football player must make that fast pass 30 yards downfield between two defenders. If they miss even a little, the ball is intercepted. If they make it, the crowd cheers because, in their hearts, they understand what a risk such a play was, and they love to see it happen, especially in American culture. And the great gambler sitting on a pile of money pushes in enough chips to take out everyone else at the table. If they miss, they may empower the winner to stick around longer. The other gunman is just as scared, just as in doubt of the outcome. So why let off the gas? Drive home the shot with a bit of fanfare and banter. When both draw and fire, there will be a winner and loser. The more committed you are, the more times you will win those engagements, so don't hold back out of fear.

Greatness isn't determined by the safe and timid; it's always made by those boldest willing to put it all on the line for what they think is the best chance. Most of the time, the other competitors won't be so persistent that some little doubt will drive them toward a mistake, which fuels great acts. Playing tight does not make anything great. It might show diligence and care, but it will not draw applause, and let's face it. When in business, the ability to live to see another day at the deal table means you need to have your fair share of applause from peers and enemies. And when you no longer get those accolades, you could figure yourself to be on the way out. If you lose your nerve, you are finished. If you get comfortable with a nice income, excellent meals, and the bootlickers who are permanently attached to success, and you stop pushing the chips into the middle of the table, that is the day that you start to become a loser.

CHAPTER NOTES:

a. In poker, at some point in the game, you have to push up your bets. You can't just sit back and rest on your winnings. Protecting your investments is not a game-winning strategy.
b. Most people in their life fold at the end of every hand because they play everything too safe.
c. Most people in business playing with house money think they are doing good to protect that money. That is why they fail so often; they do not make those risky bets when they should have. Losers cave to the pressure of the bets.
d. Gunfighting and poker playing are very similar; both bet on the outcomes favoring the bold, playing highs against the lows. At some point in every game, you have to know when to place a bet and act on it.

THE OBSCURITY OF LEADERSHIP

Of course, the point of playing cards in the first place coming out of France and migrating into the United States during the days of piracy, revolution then the Civil War was to "play the courts." The queen, jack, and king cards were similar to the origins of chess in that the players "played" the courts and the political elements for victory or defeat. Success in the games was getting the kings and queens to do what we wanted them to do for a strategic outcome. In that regard, playing cards were very much part of the revolutionary period where the mind of humanity began to divorce itself away from royal worship. Looking at poker cards from L.I. Cohen printed in 1864, the royal cards were depicted with tiny hands and feet a year before the Civil War ended. Mocking royal courts was the fashion of the day because, in New York, where the cards were designed and printed, individualism was very much on everyone's mind, and in leisure, mockery of such ancient thinking was the trend.

Royal mockery is essential in modern business because that same sentiment is still quite prevalent to this very day. When employees view their leadership, it is naturally with resistance toward authority. However, in business, the challenge of leadership is to overcome this natural resistance to rule without destroying the people in the process, which can be a very tricky matter. The people working for an organization don't and won't automatically follow whoever is the designated authority figure. Resentment toward any authority, specifically in America, is natural and nurtured for many centuries in a straightforward trajectory. It won't be un-invented with some simplistic charts and name play options created by the bounty hunters in the field. The real players of the game have to win by letting the players play themselves and switching the nature of the objectives around so that the natural inclination of the participants is harnessed without destroying them.

The day's trend that won't be going away soon is for the leadership to dress down and show the employees that they are ordinary people and not above the workers' station. Peer pressure has done this, which isn't what the employees want at all. Often, they want to be led, but they don't want that leader to be a stuffy desk-driven monarch who inherited the position out of bootlicking and favoritism. They want their leaders to be the best of the best. If such a person proves themselves worthy, workers are willing to follow them to the ends of the earth. But the leader can't be a fake.

Going back to the sentiments of the gunfighter, once they had a reputation of killing a few bandits, word would get around, and before they knew it, they were the sheriff of the town. People would follow the sheriff/gunfighter because of the reputation they had. Without a reputation, people resent the leadership. Everyone despises leadership by title, and it has been for centuries, going back to every royal court that ever existed. When human beings found a way to break themselves free of that relationship, they did so, and their games reflected that sentiment. In the world of modern business leadership, the rules of engagement are no less and are very well known.

Leaders who don't understand the game seek to appease their employees with open-neck polo shirts and even present knowledge of current events around the water cooler. They want to be liked by their employees because they don't have a reputation that creates respect, so they attempt to fake the sentiment to justify their position. The results are disastrous for everyone involved because nobody is getting what they want; a decisive leader will stand stoic in the face of fire and take on all challengers without fail. That is the kind of behavior that earns the right to have a corner office and respect from their workers. Not the loser who pretends to be a leader when, in fact, all they are could be summed up with the jack card in any poker deck from 1864, tiny feet, tiny hands, and tiny minds.

I have personally found it amazing how willing people are to call you "boss" once you have proven yourself to have a reputation worthy of the title. When people say "my boss," they often indicate a person they act on behalf of and want to feel good about it. So it is up to leadership to give them something to believe in, to refer to their boss with pride and honor. The worst thing a boss could do is be the kind of person who does not inspire greatness, be some crybaby complaining about their many toils in life, and show fear when a gunfighter is needed to face a threat alone in a dusty street. Being called a boss has always made me feel uncomfortable because I never liked calling anybody that term since I have always been on the leadership side of things naturally. It is not something I enjoy doing, giving other people possession of my life, so by default, I have always been that person in the dusty street facing down whatever threat there was. But for most people, they don't want to be that person; they want a boss who will, or otherwise, a sheriff to act on their behalf.

Leadership isn't complicated; it is born out of honor and courage. In every case where a chain of command is instituted to simulate some ancient royal court behavior, natural resentments become the dominating aspect of any culture. The business endeavor becomes much less effective. In the times of the gunfighter, leadership was established when a challenge was issued. And that challenge was met with action. Many institutions call barbaric the ways and means of personal duels; it remains the primary exhibitor of leadership in any culture.

When playing card games like poker, the trend was to poke fun literally at the royal elements. The game players were putting themselves above those previously respected layers of life and manipulating them toward personal advantage. That behavior was more than just a game; it was a psychological transition from a passive subservient to an active leader. While it's true that most people don't crave to be leaders themselves, they at least want to follow the one they can believe in, and for those leaders, the title has to be earned, not just applied. There is no escaping the human mind's desire for leadership, and those who present themselves as leaders will have to face down some danger equivalent at some point in their life, or at many times, a gunfight against a dangerous foe. Such confrontations can be terminal, but they are necessary because they are brought into the world. They can't be purchased at a university or applied by force through some government. Leaders are forged under pressure and danger, and every business environment in the world is looking for a good leader. And every worker in those places is too. Leadership is one of the rarest things globally, but they are the greatest gift humanity could hope for when it is made.

CHAPTER NOTES:

a. Card games reflected the ability of the players to manipulate the courts of traditional European society. The idea of controlling royal worship was the beginning of a divorce where Americans separated from the aristocracy of the homeland.
b. The challenge of leadership is to convince people to follow without the resentment built into the history of authority.
c. Many managers fail to appeal to their employees by pandering to them by dressing down and trying to appear like an everyday person. This, of course, is not what people want to follow.
d. Leadership by title is not authentic. Leadership is earned, not issued. When people call you boss, it is out of pride, not respect for a crown.

IT'S ALL ABOUT PREPARATION

As every great gunfighter knows, the wins don't come from luck or just wake up one day and be faster to the draw and eliminate your enemies as they present themselves. The wins come from the countless hours you spend working with your guns, cleaning them, listening to how they work, and essentially knowing them inside and out. That way, when the time comes, you work the gun like it's part of your own body, and it does what you command seamlessly. The muscle memory in your hands knows every small measurement on the gun, and the weight of it loaded and unloaded is easy to detect with your eyes closed. That way, when you must have that standoff against an aggressor, you aren't surprised by anything, and your mind is free to take care of that task at hand. Only a fool would wake up one morning and think that they would survive an upcoming gunfight without having the small details of the event memorized as a second nature, which is the road to any measure of success in almost every occupation.

In business, we have the same concerns, only it's not a lead bullet that we are concerned with, but often other equally dangerous elements that can ruin you in the blink of an eye if not handled correctly. Such a scenario would be the simple sending of an email, but you are trying to answer your phone while sending it, you are late for an important meeting, and there are people outside of your office wanting your attention. The email is time-sensitive, so you have to get it out, but you can't remember the email address since it's a new contact and you don't yet have it in your address book. All this is going on simultaneously, and your success that day requires you to do everything well. The significant risk is that while you go through old emails looking for that contact info, you need that while in a hurry; you might send the wrong email to the wrong recipient, especially if you are working with several different customers. The matter gets even more complicated if you are working with different cultures all around the world. It is easy to send the wrong information to the wrong recipient, especially if the names are similar, such as you might have a Sarah in London or a Sarah in Australia. Or perhaps even a Saka in Japan. By just hitting "S," you might miss that the wrong contact comes up on your email while under duress, and the result could be just as bad as a death in a gunfight. The consequences of that failure could be just as terminal. Sometimes living with a significant mistake in life may be worse than a terminal encounter because you'll have to live with it for the rest of your life.

The best argument for the modern businessperson is to spend time at the gun range learning to handle firearms, not just in shooting into a target but also in loading and unloading a gun while others are shooting around you. For instance, some weapons others are firing are very powerful, and they put out quite a concussion of power when they are discharged, making it so that it is difficult to think in the next lane over if you are not used to those forces. Of course, these are not significant issues for a seasoned shooter, but for a novice just learning to shoot or might come to the range with frazzled nerves, it can be quite a jolt. Learning to deal with that jolt is why it is good to practice shooting. In every good gun range, many rules must be followed, so the process of shooting can organize your thoughts. The level of danger with guns is great because if someone on the range makes a mistake, it could be dangerous for everyone. Being aware of your potential for errors is not enough; looking out for the mistakes of others is just as important. All those elements make a better mind to conduct business in regular life because the same characteristics apply.

Being a business leader, the daily pressures are not so different, so it is my experience that learning to shoot guns at a range well helps prepare the mind for the rigors of the business world. It is pretty common to look at businesspeople as a pampered class of desk sitters who don't do much because that is how our culture has allowed themselves to think of that occupation. In truth, if done correctly, the pressure of business is quite ominous, and not everyone handles the pressures well, which is why health risks and other stress-related factors often come into play when discussing businesspeople and their practices. Under the best of conditions, even if a business leader does their job well, most people won't appreciate it, and the results are often not seen by many people even though they benefit from the success. Just like in shooting, a good day at the range is usually only known by the shooter. It is true; it is lonely at the top; get used to it. Most people in the world won't have any idea how or why something was successful. Coming to terms with that reality is one of the great benefits of learning to shoot firearms under any condition, especially Cowboy Fast Draw, where pressure, speed, and the muscle memory of thousands and thousands of shots have forged you into a speed and accuracy machine.

Such was the tradition of the gunfighter; few people cared if they lived or died, most people didn't like them—that is until they faced down someone everyone else feared more. Upon a successful gun battle where the gunfighter won, they might be considered heroes, but not for long. Appreciation usually dies away quickly, and people resort back to their comforts until the next crisis, which the gunfighter may or may not be ready when the next time occurs. Due to the nature of living life in such a way, always being prepared for danger, never getting comfortable with everyday living, alcohol and reckless living often killed the gunfighter before a bullet ever did. So it is with most business people functioning at a high level for all the same reasons.

Learning to shoot and working with guns is a great way to come to terms with these elements of risk and preparation. Whether in the occupation of a gunfighter or as a businessperson. Dealing with escalating interest rates and the pressures of P&L demands can be just as scary as a posse of armed thugs rolling into town to bring fear and loathing in their wake. When that pressure hits, you need to function under pressure without sending the wrong email to the inappropriate contact or tipping off those who need your attention that you are under stress and not someone they can depend on to lead them. They don't want to see you sweat; they want to know you can handle anything. So, if you are in a business leadership position, or you want to be, then don't make mistakes under pressure. Be so well prepared for everything through lots of practice and repetition that you can do the everyday things very quickly because you have done them in practice thousands of times, even if the practice is as common as sending an email. Treat every shot as dangerous, be mindful of the risks, and never take anything for granted, especially on the shooting range. Preparing in such a way will lead to great success not just on the shooting range but also from behind your desk.

CHAPTER NOTES:

a. Wins in life come from countless hours of preparation, such as in shooting. Knowing everything on a gun through muscle memory by working diligently with them is the way to success in everything.
b. Under pressure in an office environment, working tasks as a second nature due to great preparation prevents mistakes.
c. Going to the gun range and dealing with the loud noises and vibrations of recoil can clear a mind rattled through stress. Learning to manage those elements makes a daily life able to endure more under pressure.
d. It is lonely at the top. Most people will never know what you did to become so good. But you will know, and others will marvel at your abilities. And that's what eventually counts.

DIFFICULTY IS MEANT TO BE OVERCOME

One thing about business is that it is constantly moving; it seldom stays in a fixed format. From year one of a person's life in business to year thirty or forty, many things will change, and it is up to the successful people to ride that change or drive it accordingly. That is why the period of American history where some of the most significant changes occurred is a good model for analysis and metaphorical assistance. In the period of the gunfighters, a change occurred almost daily, from rustic towns occurring all over the West overnight shortly after the end of the Civil War to bustling metropolises that suddenly came to life with electricity. Ironically as technology improved, human independence lessened, which was the cause of many of the significant conflicts that became legends during the age of the gunfighters. Yet without the gunfighters, America would have completely lost its soul during this time in history. There are reasons that people who tell stories about Butch Cassidy or Jessie James want to believe that they escaped some tragic shootout and lived out their days happy and wise from their riches acquired as outlaws. There is always hope that a human being can become something better than a compliant subservient by being an outlaw. The actual path to innovation began when outlaws plotted with great ambition to rob trains and banks instead of stringing electricity along railroad tracks to bring a new level of civilization to the antics of imagination.

When a new project is started in a business enterprise, there are always those who proclaim how difficult everything will be. They, after all, like the world they were living in and comfortable with the rules they understand, come to a comfortable level of complacency. Change means new rules will come about and more things for them to pay attention to, so of course, there will always be anxiety. And each time there is something new that comes along, all the new elements bring new skills to learn, which can be very daunting. Managing difficulty is why shooting sports are terrific devices for keeping a business mind sharp and flexible enough to incorporate new conduct for treasure hunting success.

Specifically, shooting sports, unlike other kinds of leisure activity, there are so many varieties of guns and ways of putting bullets into targets that the variability itself does a mind a lot of good in using that method to teach itself how to adapt to change. With each new gun that a shooter utilizes, from all the different pistol calibers with various barrel lengths to the rifles, shotguns, and modern semi-automatics, dozens and dozens of multiple competitions have arisen to utilize all the options. Even seasoned shooters struggle to learn new competitive events and find it very hard to learn new skills. Most people in life learn one thing here and there, then stop once they are comfortable. But the best shooters learn many new skills with many new calibers and styles of weapons. And it is that approach that is needed in business when undertaking new endeavors.

Eventually, with any practice, what seems very hard at first becomes much easier over time. Once a challenger has put in enough time into learning, skills become much more obtainable, which is undoubtedly the case with each new business project. When starting, everyone may understand the nature of the endeavor, such as shooting a new gun. The purpose of a gun is to fire projectiles at a target, whether near or far; it doesn't matter. The function is what is consistent. In business, it is to make a product and provide it to the market in some profitable format.

The experienced leader, just like the professional gunfighter, knows that with some diligence, they can trust in skill development and not surrender their ambitions to self-doubt. When shooting a new gun in a new format, they understand how to tweak the environmental conditions to become successful. Business is no different; a person successful in their history may get a new challenge and struggle with it for a short time as they learn the applicable conditions under the circumstances. However, with some practice, they soon learn to perform well and find that everything gets easier for them once they master the basic skills of the endeavor.

Too often, when a new business need is enacted, it starts with very enthusiastic salespeople who are eager for something new, such as buying a new gun. But when it comes time to shoot the gun, they find a lot more recoil than they thought there would be, and soon after that, they find the whole exchange intimidating. But once they push through and learn to make the recoil adjustments and aren't flinching when they pull the trigger so much, their shots are much more manageable, and their ability to hit the target is more conducive to success. Such as it is in business when a new project is unleashed, and at first, everyone reels from the new skills needed to become good. But it doesn't take long to master the new elements if only diligence is applied and a positive attitude toward the learning curve is evident.

Those who fail at life are the same as those shooters who shoot a gun and find the recoil scary, and they put it down and don't try again. Or those who see other shooters performing their craft very fast and accurately think they could never achieve such a thing. When things get hard in business, that is not the time to put the guns away and do something else. That is when practice and skill must be developed until comfort with the guns is achieved. And that is the difference between success and failure. Success isn't always about having the best skill from the start but having the willingness to learn and overcome opposition. For the same reasons that there weren't many great gunfighters, there aren't many great business leaders because the skills of overcoming opposition are the same. It's not enough to have a gun; one could not call themselves a gunfighter unless they knew how to use that gun under duress against a challenge. And the same in business, it's more than just wearing a tie or a suit to an important meeting. You don't necessarily have to know all the game rules, but you do have to have the heart to learn along the way and work hard enough at practice to become good. Surprisingly, most businesspeople yield to challenges making it so that with just that little bit of extra effort, it is not difficult to dominate a particular field because many will push through a new skill to add it to their experience. Like the lonely gunfighter when everything was much more structured without the busyness of electricity, the field of business is more of a lost art than a common practice.

It takes work to be good at it, and that is something most of your rivals won't be willing to do, which leaves many unanswered opportunities for the taking.

CHAPTER NOTES:

a. Business never stays in a fixed format; it is up to people to adapt to that change.
b. There is always hope that a human being can become something more than a servant to institutionalism. This is why people like outlaws.
c. Change always means learning something new, and many people fear this because they don't want to do more work in their life.
d. The experienced leader trusts that skill development is the key to fulfillment and is not burdened by self-doubt invoked through changes they aren't prepared for.

LESS THAN THE BLINK OF AN EYE

I have had the unique opportunity to be involved in timed weapons activity for many years now, most recently with Cowboy Fast Draw, but before that, we did in Ohio an event called Bullwhip Fast Draw. At an annual event called the Annie Oakley Festival, we had a bullwhip-heavy competition for an audience in the old Buffalo Bill Wild West Show-style tradition. At this event I have participated in since the early 2000s, the Ohio Fast Draw Association held an annual shoot next to our area, so there was a lot of fast draw going on that involved someone saying "go" then some quick activity to hit a target in front of an audience. I learned many essential lessons in doing this over the years, which essentially became this book's contents.

Under pressure, I have tried various ways to prepare for these events, which I would say are distinctly familiar to all participants. With the Bullwhip Fast Draw, a distinctly Ohio thing, meaning it's not done anywhere else in the world, I have managed to gain some level of success directly applied to my pursuits in Cowboy Fast Draw. There is no way to hide from it because it is put there under pressure, but the reaction time from the start and end of the matches is directly applicable to how success is applied to business or failure is realized. And it all comes down to those first moments before someone either says "draw" or a light comes on indicating that it is time to hit the target with your weapon. In those moments of eternity, while you are waiting, much of the success or failure is determined, and it is worth study.

I have tried many ways of dealing with the pressure. In the least successful times, I stood at the line in a kind of meditative reaction to the world around me, trying to quiet down the noise and be ultra-relaxed. A relaxed state often has cost me somewhere between .250 of a second to .300. For most people, the blink of an eye is somewhere between .300 to .400 of a second. But in these fast draw activities, that is an eternity. Once you train your mind to think that fast, you will learn to feel the difference of a .100 of a second. And in that time, if there is doubt in your thoughts, it will directly transfer over into this fast draw objective. When I have been very successful with a fast draw, I have looked forward to hitting the target with an almost spring-loaded ambition, which directly translates to saving that .300 of a second of indecision generally occupied by a completely relaxed mind. The mental state is often the difference between success and failure in fast draw activities and life.

In these events, moments before the indicator announces the time to draw, anxiety creeps in. It forces you to go from a relaxed state into action so quickly that the mind almost rebels at the activity. It is the complete opposite of the skills needed for sleep or meditation, where emptying your mind of thoughts is the optimal thing to do. In the case of a fast draw, you want to load your mind up with aggression and ambition. When the time comes, you want to attack the target free of opposition, and that is how you can know faster than the blink of an eye that you will win that match. You don't want to be thinking, "oh no, oh no, oh no, there it is," then draw and fire. You want to be thinking, "I can't wait, I can't wait, now, now now," Fire! That is how you win at these things, and through practice, you learn to think in that fast fashion that is needed in milliseconds.

Looking forward to the target is directly applicable in the business world many times a day. For instance, you know that a phone call is coming that will be dreadful, you don't want to talk to the other person. You can approach the matter with dread consuming each moment before the call is made with those "I want to get this over with, but I never want the phone to ring" kind of thinking, or you can approach it in the way you need to with fast draw targets—training yourself to look forward to the engagement. How you answer the phone and how quickly the thoughts come to your mind once you are in the conversation will largely determine the success or failure of the call.

Or consider those trips to human resources where some dreadful meeting is set up, and you are making the long walk to have the exchange. You should not wait until the last minute, stopping at every distraction you can find from wherever you came from to the destination; you should be loaded like a spring to do whatever you need to do. Thinking in this fashion will bring words faster to your mind when you need them and keep you off your heels when it matters most. The same holds of other meetings in the variety that come in business, from customer interactions to internal discussions, fast decisions are best. When words need to go quickly in your mind, and your performance is judged on speed and content, you want to be leaning into the targets, not sitting back on your heels. Often the thought process of communicating and going through the vast catalog of thoughts in your head that are needed, usually in a fraction of a second, will determine how successful you are in every outcome. So in that way, training yourself in these fast draw arts has a natural ability to increase the speed and manner of your thinking under all stressful circumstances.

In the ways of the gunfighter at the draw of a gun, life or death was the outcome; life could flash before the participants' eyes. A bit of doubt left to linger in those milliseconds before the action took place. And in that instant, wins and losses are always determined. Whether it was a gunfight in the street during Western Expansion or a challenger in the boardroom always associated with corporate life. Reacting to the speed of necessity will make all the difference in the world; thinking fast and having the desire to hit your target is the way to win, not contemplating some relaxed state of existence among the world's noise. That is not the way of the fast draw in the Western world, which is not the way to win at life. You cannot approach your targets with dread or anxiety but with eagerness and ambition. You should look forward to the word "draw" or the light in Cowboy Fast Draw. And when you train your mind in such a way, in every part of your life, especially in business, you will find that your mind is faster and sharper in the blink of an eye needed to make wins more common and losing the other person's problem.

CHAPTER NOTES:

a. Under the pressure of timed competitions, a business mind can practice the needed skills daily in regular life activities. Shooting sports are great ways to push yourself in managing pressure.
b. Once you train your mind to think fast, you will see the differences in small amounts of time measured. What might seem impossible untrained is possible once trained. Meditation is not the way to attack a target. A loaded approach is.
c. Looking forward to a target takes away the reluctance that can profoundly affect performance. Don't allow dread to consume your decision-making process.
d. Don't approach your targets on your heels; lean into them and look forward to the exchange. That is the way to win.

GIFTS BORN FROM FREEDOM

Thinking of places like Dodge City and Deadwood, which were seething with scum and villainy during the Old West period, many comparable considerations are directly applicable to modern business. There is an incorrect assumption that with more rules and regulations, an improvement in output is the byproduct. The opposite is true. Much of what we consider the "romance" of the Old West period came not from the lack of showers, an abundance of prostitutes, deadly gun encounters, diseases, alcoholism, and general corruption that permeated such early towns, but in the opportunities that drove their populations. Many say that the Wild West was built on "greed," which is a lazy way of pinpointing human ambition. Most people are driven by what they can acquire for themselves, which defines a good life. In the period of Western Expansion, those ambitions were cut loose. People were free to step out of some station that had limited their families for thousands of years and become independently wealthy or die trying.

That same sentiment is on full display in the modern era, especially in places like Las Vegas, a boomtown founded for all the same reasons that Dodge City and Deadwood rose to fame. It is ironic that once electricity and order came to much of the West, we kept a lot of that spirit alive in Las Vegas as Americans. Modern businesspeople attending a convention in Las Vegas have all the optimism that used to be present in gold prospecting in Deadwood. Any new business contact or even some side occurrence in a casino might change their lives forever in the blink of an eye. Most visitors in Vegas will come away with regrets and a lot of lost money, but the promise of some opportunity for riches keeps people coming back and hoping.

In Deadwood, Seth Bullock was a merchant who took up a gun to bring some order and justice to that Sin City of the Blackhills. What stood in the way of complete mayhem and stifling rules was the gunfighter turned sheriff who could keep the roads coming into the town open for trade, staving off the bandits and thieves looking for a quick get wealthy plan at the expense of others. Once civilization had taken over in these places, their excitement disappeared into history, and it could be argued that they were greatly diminished. Sure, all the vile things were put to order, the prostitution was shut down, the gangs of thugs vanquished, the gambling eliminated—but so were all the opportunities for individuals to become personally wealthy during a boom time. Understanding the need for reckless abandon being at the center of most innovation, the modern city of Las Vegas in American culture was set aside to be that place from our past where such opportunities could still exist.

When I think of Las Vegas, I think of daredevils like Evel Knievel jumping the Caeser's Palace fountains and crashing, then many other stunt performers attempting it and succeeding. I think of great restaurants like those from Gordon Ramsey, the famous television star who has raised a refined dining profile in Vegas. I think of the many performers who make good livings doing live shows that are pretty extraordinary, everything from the Osmonds to Blue Man Group. Then, all the degradation elements usually present when morality is tossed out the window and pleasures are put in front of practicality. It is not a surprise that so many business conventions make their home in Las Vegas because the place inspires opportunity, and that has always been the name of the game.

While the economy of Dodge City was built on the buying of buffalo skins primarily so that the Indians of that region would lose their food supply, the opportunity for the buffalo hunters to get rich on the practice had not existed before. The Indians certainly didn't have such an arrangement as their view of life was in harmony with nature. When the Western civilization that came to the Dodge City area and decided to pay for buffalo hides to the point where that species nearly went extinct provided an opportunity to those willing to brave the conditions to improve their lives. Not to live within the parameters of nature, which is at the heart of all business activity. The morality of that enterprise depends on one's world outlook, yet the circumstances of human learning are universal. Most people just want to improve their lives somehow, which is the lesson to learn from these examples.

When running a business or managing employees within the context of a corporation, it is essential to understand this trait. The need for people to have opportunities is far more critical than the boundaries of rules and regulations. Most people would prefer to be an outlaw than a moral and upright contributor to society if only they could leave their station in life and enjoy the fruits of prosperity, if only for an evening. People will throw caution entirely into the wind braving diseases and poor health to taste the unlimited boundaries of opportunity for a moment. With that in mind, it is up to the enterprising manager to show employees the opportunities that await them rather than force them into a compliance culture that will stifle their creativity and rob them of the motivations needed to take whatever endeavor the business is concerned with to the next level.

Business conventions in Las Vegas hold within them a reckless ambition for the possible, and that value system is far more motivating than a long list of rules meant to withhold conduct to a set standard. Left to their own devices, people will always choose the reckless and tragic if there is even a remote possibility of touching freedom even once in their lives. That is the lesson to understand people: they will choose villainy for a chance at personal freedom. A good businessperson understands this notion and utilizes it for good, which often means a sense of justice is best unleashed when personal growth and opportunity are well defined for employees so that they can enjoy the fruits of their labors.

The tragedies often associated with Western Expansion are defined in the context of rules, whether those rules were created by eastern thinking Indians trying to live in harmony with nature or by governments looking to be the next power player on the world stage. Individual people care what happens to them, and when they see the opportunity for gains that might change their lives forever come about, they will do just about anything and risk a great deal to touch it for a second. Only the threat of death tames their restless spirits, certainly not the rules of civilization. The brilliant strategist understands these forces and puts them into balance, especially in the practice of business.

The intelligent businessperson going to Vegas to network with peers may ponder with great mystery why their co-workers and subordinates roam the city at night searching for trouble. Still, understanding why they do what they do is the first significant step in leading them. People only follow compliance so long as it connects them toward opportunity. And the only real motivator that governs proper behavior when reckless abandon is ruling the minds of the masses is the promise of pain and death because that puts away any future opportunities for some taste of personal freedom.

CHAPTER NOTES:

a. There is an incorrect assumption that more rules and regulations will improve output.
b. Most people are driven by what they can acquire for themselves. And for a chance at it, they will commit incredible feats of good or villainy. Whatever it takes to gain freedom and autonomy.
c. The need for reckless abandon is the driver of most innovation, so it is good to facilitate as much of it that can be conducted without destroying a culture.
d. To have success is in management finding a way to join employees to the fruits of prosperity, to utilize their need for personal fulfillment with the requirements of a business.

THE SNAKE BITE OF JEALOUSY

In many ways, there is a hatred of businesspeople that runs hand in hand with the sentiments used to accompany the Wild West gunfighter. Even today, when a businessperson on their way to work dressed in attire consistent with professionalism goes into a gas station, people quickly open doors for them out of respect. Behind that sentiment is a cutting hatred that is persistent with modern thinking. Just as people loved the stories of gunfighters and their antics, they hated the people who stood between them and wickedness for reasons that defy logic, only in that the tides of independence for which all people respond also have the programmed desire to return to the sea. The gunfighter, then the businessperson who followed, stands against that retreat, and for that trait, there is much quiet hatred.

The modern businessperson must be comfortable with this hatred. Within their organizations, there will always be others looking to tear them down. There are rivalries for power and prestige among their peers, and of course, out in the world, there is the same hatred that talks about Wall Street as if it were an evil entity of vast conspiracy. The businessperson must function independently of these forces and find themselves like the Old West's gunfighters in that everywhere they turn, there is a danger likely undeserved. A natural reaction to this sentiment is to become defensive and look at all the danger and feel its pressure and allow it to define you. The best of the gunfighters from the past embraced that hatred and turned it to their advantage on most occasions, which the modern businessperson should do.

The reason that doors open when you dress formally is that people respect anything that goes above and beyond the required effort. When a gunfighter officially dressed in the streets of a raging boomtown filled with tired, dusty merchants and traders, they displayed that they were above the station of chaos. Their guns and cards had earned them the ability to do more with their day than merely survive. For instance, Wild Bill was known for his excellent attire and routine of bathing every day, not the usual practice at the time. The well-dressed had displayed that the wearer had not only just survived but had done much more above that objective. And this is the source of the hatred. It's not the gunfighter, or the modern businessperson hated at face value for an honest assessment. It is what such a person represents to the lazy and unambitious which is the source of the problem.

A businessperson represents ambition and purpose. The very nature of business is to make something and to sell it to someone who needs it, yet most people only wish to have a meal in their lives and some leisure time to watch the sunset. If they do anything beyond that, they talk about the people doing things because they don't dare to do them themselves. People do respect a well-dressed businessperson. The businessperson represents ambition and an unsatisfied version of world events. While that is an admirable trait, it also reminds others that they do not have the same aspirations and lack the courage to change their present circumstances.

The businessperson must embrace that controversy and feed off it. The pull of history's tides is trying to stop progress and innovation. In many ways, being a businessperson is more art than function, as what is made and sold is a product of imagination and desire. For the businessperson who brings a new restaurant to town, the many challenges that must be conquered to do so are enormous. First, an establishment must be found or built, then a supply chain to deliver the food. Then, of course, a customer base must be constructed and maintained. Between each of those steps are hundreds if not thousands of micro-decisions that must be made to keep such a place open under the best circumstances. Of course, there will come the shakedowns from the political class, who want to attach themselves to success but have every desire to extort wealth from every enterprise to sustain their own needs for power, only without building anything. Then consider all the various types of businesses, it's one thing to talk about a restaurant because everyone must eat. Think of all the companies that offer unique items, like certain kinds of clothes or books. The more unique, the harder it is to build a market for them. It takes a lot of work to do anything in business, so what is always behind the anger directed at business people, whether from Wall Street movers and shakers or the local merchant, is that people are jealous of the results unwilling to do the work themselves. The businessperson represents ambition and hard work which is a reminder that everyone else is underperforming.

The early gunfighters of the American frontier worked harder than others to have the courage to face down danger where it presented itself. They worked harder to acquire skills and wealth that would even put a good gun in their hands, so wearing a weapon projected a successful acquisition of power to purchase such a thing and then defend their independence with it. Many people admire such efforts at face value, but upon their reflection, they feel the sting of guilt from their lackluster actions, so their sentiments develop into jealousy and hatred.

That is why modern businesspeople and gunfighters have so much in common. We may have replaced the guns for neckties and high heels, but the effects and judgments are the same. Businesspeople are not happy with how the world is; they are always looking to improve it, grow, build wealth, and use that wealth to alter the world further. Most are happy watching the ebbs and flows of life move in and out like the waters of a beach, not motivated to play much of a part. High tides bring all the sea's riches; then, as the moon passes behind the earth, the wave moves back out, taking with it all it brought forth. Most people are happy with this relationship until the businessperson captures the contents and keeps them once the sea retreats, and now an effort is required to stand against nature. The very act of business, or defending oneself with a gun, is to change the state of nature and protect the gains made with ambition and imagination. Not to yield to nature and accept the fate that is given to us all. When a businessperson dresses up to conduct themselves, they announce to the world that they are not satisfied with nature and have a mind to change it. And for the lazy who wish to exist, that is a slight to their decisions. While they may be too lazy to do anything about their feelings, they still develop those dark clouds for which their eyes reveal that inner hatred for the businessperson—and all who display ambition proudly. Yet like the gunfighters, the modern businessperson must learn to embrace such controversy because it is a good indicator that success is brewing and riches are on the horizon.

CHAPTER NOTES:

a. There is a natural hatred of businesspeople that permeates society in general. The cutting emotions reside in the understanding that a successful person stands against the retreat of the lazy toward regression.
b. The businessperson must see themselves in the lonely fashion of the American gunfighter, who function on their intuition and advantage.
c. To present themselves above the station of chaos, a gunfighter and modern businessperson display that they represent ambition and purpose. They raise the bar for those who would rather keep it low.
d. A businessperson is a representative of art in that they represent hopes and dreams driven by ambition which is a product of imagination. Those who don't have a purpose don't want the reminder of their failures.

ICE WATER IN THE SUMMER

When the great gunfighter and sheriff, Bat Masterson, died over his typewriter reflecting on his many days as a lawman, he left behind an important message for the future. He had spent a life keeping the Wild West manageable as an opportunity for all; his last words were, "the rich man gets his ice in the summer, the poor man in the winter." To me, this was one of the wisest statements in the history of the world. It captured the essence of the intent of modern economies, for which every business plays a part. The goal of an economy driven by free enterprise is to find markets in need by supplying goods and services that people value, such as the ability to get ice anytime, anyplace in our modern age. In the times of Bat Masterson, at the start of the 20th century, there was a good reason that people went West and it was to gain the ability to have ice water in the summer, to become a rich person, and to for the first time in their lives step beyond the confines of nature.

Getting rich has a negative connotation formed over many years by those who would prefer the limits of nature instead of their conquest. The American West was freeing people to get rich without social station if they could brave the elements and survive long enough to gain some wealth. For most, they would die trying, or they would end up more impoverished than they started. But the opportunity to have a shot at wealth, to have a shot at ice water in the summer when the concept of refrigeration wasn't even yet a fantasy meant that very enterprising individuals were unleashed to change the course of the human race forever.

That was the most significant contribution of the Wild West gunfighter, that unlike the unorganized period of history involving piracy during the romantic period of the late 1600s. Romantic because of the concepts of individualism developed during that period, not due to the death, carnage, and even cannibalism that took place in the many scourges of the sea. Shortly after that, during the opening of the wild frontier in America, during the mid-1700s, great individualists like Daniel Boone and Simon Kenton tamed the Ohio territory down into what we call Tennessee today, where the ideas for America were born. It was innovation against nature, the gunfighters against the Indians, and obviously, the Indians lost. There was naturally lots of sorrow and trauma, but for what end? The frontiersman's answer was freedom at all costs; then, the gunfighter followed the American businessperson's desire for independence and ice water goal in the summer.

For many centuries prior, food, shelter, and any luxury item such as a bed or a table were the state's products. You were either in with a king's court, or you were barely hanging on for dear life as a peasant farmer. The age of piracy, then the frontiersman followed by the Wild West gunfighter, paved a path that allowed for the building of the railroads and the tremendous businesses that erupted along the new supply chains that connected the Pacific Ocean with the Atlantic. Once the regional governors, the kings, the noble landowners of Europe, and the Orient were left behind and free people were left to their courage and imaginations, inventions like refrigeration were created to sustain those ambitions. While the game of poker was being invented in New Orleans, Ferdinand Carre's new refrigeration system was a solution to that city's ice problems since the Civil War prevented them from getting ice from New England. Previously, even in New England, getting ice was costly and very difficult, Bat Masterson's quote for reference. In 1867 another French immigrant named Andrew Muhl built an ice machine to help the expanding beef industry push West.

As individual desires pushed Western Expansion the many inventions such as ice production came along with it. Soon there was electricity spanning the length of the railroads and then telephone communications. None of these things would have come about without the frontiersmen and gunfighters who removed the barriers to entry, namely nature, superstition, and the political class restrictions, which had always been a part of human development. Those exact needs still permeate all American business concepts, as the requirements and conditions for each one are the same. All markets and the needs for the markets come from freedom needing less restriction, not compliance, and more restriction. The ambitions of sales in every company are to do as much as possible in the modern world. By the time rules and regulations are applied, businesses end up with only a fraction of what they originally dreamed of bringing to market.

Modern interpretation suggests all Wild West towns were built to pursue gold and personal enrichment to the detriment of a race of people occupying the land as "natives." It is further suggested that all the drunkenness, the evils of the brothels, the general condition of the many killers and thieves were devastating. Yet no credit is given to the great benefit of ice, electricity, trains, and eventually modern living such as air conditioning, heating, stoves, beds, and even clothing made in a mass way that was born as a result. If not for the gunfighters and the enterprising businesspeople of American industry, where would the world be?

And we can see for ourselves what happens when territories do not experience their own Wild West freedom movement, places like Africa where all they see of modern luxury is imported on the back of some pickup truck by visitors from the outside. The people themselves do not have the freedom to invent, let alone find food for a day, as oppressive governments always stand in the way of personal growth and innovation. A trip to the Middle East shows the same, where there are oil markets to ship to America, there is wealth. But all other places are still stuck in the time of the Crusades as swords and sticks still define the merit of culture, always looking back, never ahead. Businesspeople who try to bring new industry to the area are either killed and picked apart by corruption because no lone gunfighters are roaming around to inflict justice. Freedom should allow individuals to build and create at will. Instead, the inhabitants of these regions stay in their homes, put curtains across their windows, and hope nobody notices them. That is why cultures do not advance in those places.

It was the gunfighter who suppressed the forces that prevent freedom, and it takes freedom to innovate. Businesses need the freedom to create new products and inspire economic growth because it has the most extraordinary morality on planet earth. There are worse things than murder and injustice; there is economic stagnation that exacerbates humanity's evils. If there had never been gunfighters and greed in the American West, the Indians would have destroyed themselves with their warring necessities, and there wouldn't be all the great things we see today in the American economy. North America would essentially look like all the other regions of the world where tyranny and stupidity are given power. People wouldn't even be concerned about having ice in the summer; they just want to live through the day. In America, because of the gunfighter and the business people, even the very poor have ice water in the summer. They can have all they can handle and more—and that in itself is a miracle of our modern times.

CHAPTER NOTES:

a. "The rich man gets his ice in the summer, the poor man in the winter," a great statement from Bat Masterson. It is the goal of capitalism and all free-market enterprise.
b. Getting rich in business is a goal to step beyond the limits of nature, which is a byproduct of nature in all human beings. To conceptualize through imagination, then through productivity, to make it so.
c. For many years prior, most assets were controlled by "state" regulators. Only when the gunfighter came on the scene was there an opportunity for free people to create solutions out of a desire to own property and drive innovation.
d. The need for accommodating the frontier beef industry drove the invention of refrigeration. Which is the case for most free-market needs in all industries.

THE BEAUTY OF RECKLESSNESS

An aspect of a business culture that is inescapable is that the nature of growth tends to destroy the type of people who started the creation in the first place. Long before the dandies moved into a town like Deadwood or any other goldrush establishment, the brave and reckless punched their way through untamed forests and wilderness perils to stake an anchor in the ground and declare with all the emphasis of a pronoun, that where they stood was "mine." It took those types of people to voyage to any new land once it was discovered, and it will take those types to venture into space for which we are on the precipice currently. It's not the organized dandies that ignite creation. Of course, they have a role in the whole adventure process, but it is nowhere near the same. This is often why the Wild West gunfighter drank themselves to death once a town was established and there was no more horizon left for them to chase. Gunfighters may have tried to get married and have children attending church on Sundays, but the best parts of their character often rot in peace when action is not required. The same forces which allowed them to face down a villain threatening to shoot them dead if only they were fast enough are the same that rots them when times of peace come. With nowhere to go, they hit the bottle and reckless lifestyles as a way of actually trying to live.

With every company that was ever made, the cycles of a wild West town can be found. Always, in the beginning, are big, bold ideas that take great courage to endure. Every company has a story about its boom period because it takes something special to make anything from nothing. Salespeople like snake oil salesman and traveling gunfighters often have a terrible reputation for being untrustworthy because the emphasis is always on what could be, not necessarily what is. To start a business, the question must be asked by some bold person what could be. Then it takes greed, honor, and sheer bravery to climb out on a limb, get money from a bank to start the business, hire people, build a team that can make the vision happen, then hope that you can get to market before the market kills you, literally. There always seem to be wild stories of business owners in their early days who wrecked sports cars and chased too many relationships in pursuit of comfort in the same ways that people talked about gunfighters and their reckless charades.

It wasn't by any kind of accident that gunfighters who might have been considered violent killers would take up the sheriff's badge once a town needed such a person. Personal survival required them to continue to use their skills of reckless abandon for the ambitions of justice. After all, the dandies needed protections as they moved in and built industry off the backs of bravery, often crushing those who came before them with stifling rules and regulations. At least the sheriff could shoot someone now and again. The danger was still part of the life of the law, so an occupation in that direction was a good choice.

Flamboyance and mayhem are precisely the traits that an upstart organization desires to give birth to something that later might become a mass employer creating the most outstanding products of the next century. But first, a company must survive the birthing process, and for that, it takes its version of the gunfighters to lay down the law and tame the wilderness for the benefit of profit. To feed those ambitions, a certain level of pretension is of utmost necessity. Later, when the rules and modes of conduct come into play to build teams of people toward common objectives, those modes of civilized thinking will make sense. Yet, in the beginning, the timid souls who make up the dandies are not on the scene leaving only egos and raw desire to drive any trend toward growth. Greed is not a bad thing because it always inspires creation. What defines greed as bad is only about the dandies' lives who are timid and need the protections of rules to establish growth.

The desire to own or possess something with the pronoun "I" is crucial to braving the odds to make something new. Traditional gunfighters or first-generation businesspeople share that desire to make something theirs and put on it their stamp of ambition, and what is born is something new in the process. Once the growth stops where individual input propels it forward, the conflict between the gunfighters and the dandies begins and ends. The wise gunfighter or businessperson will learn to either move on to the next town that needs their unique services or becomes the sheriff and help the dandies build order. The same skills for maintaining a business are not the same ones required to make it from nothing. The two personalities rarely can live together where choices define conduct.

It is usually not heavy drinking and liaisons with the opposite sex that kill such early adventurers; it's boredom once opportunities run out. Just a quick trip around the world will show many cultures that have destroyed their flamboyant adventurers with too many rules and a blanket of social justice. And by killing those types of people before they are even out of their childhoods, there aren't enough people to build new businesses and give birth to innovation. There are plenty of obedient workers who are like the dandies and willing to punch a time clock and get paid, but there aren't enough in their populations who stay up all night building a new business and fighting for its life with all the ambitions of profit to set it loose. America still makes such people in their culture but not without some levels of controversy as the dandies have forgotten how to respect them. But at least in America, there is still a place for the gunfighter types to make a living and sustain themselves long enough for business creation.

Compliance is an absolute necessity for creating a mass culture of any kind, whether into a town turning into a city or a small business turning into a big company. Unfortunately, the skills it takes to make one into another are different. While the transition occurs, the best of the gunfighters, if they are excellent, can find a happy middle ground into law enforcement where their bravery and flamboyance still have a home. Unfortunately, many ambitious types will kill themselves with reckless lives, and the dandies will pray for their accelerated demise. The timid natures of the dandies just cannot handle the bold proclamations of the pronoun "I" when drunk and unregulated aggression confronts them on a city street. Or when their spouses are trying to sneak out the window to be near such reckless people, they are more exciting. The dandies want such people dead to free them to do their part in building a city out of the town or a big business out of the small enterprise. That makes the original gunfighter out to be more of a villain when they think they should be remembered heroes. But that is the nature of things and depending on which type you are, maybe moving to the next town is the best thing. Perhaps becoming a sheriff is. Or maybe a path to self-destruction is all that is left. But always remember that nothing would come to be without the gunfighter, and the world owes at least a little respect, even if it is under their breaths.

CHAPTER NOTES:

a. One reason gunfighters drank themselves to death, the skills needed to start something with significant risk are not the same for sustainability; they become destructive as an ill-advised way to continue living.
b. Flamboyance and mayhem are the traits that give birth to something new before the dandies come to loot off the efforts of the brave.
c. The desire to defend the pronoun "I" drives a growth culture out of a need for ownership for which order would protect.
d. Boredom kills off the gunfighters once there is no longer a need for risk and games of chance. The dandies have forgotten how to respect the birthing process for which the risk-takers performed.

INDIVIDUAL SKILL BEATS PRIMITIVE SUPERSTITION

It is certainly not the purpose of this analysis to prove that the West is better than the East in culture and general business practice. For my part, I have significantly enjoyed doing business with people from the East. They are generally very respectable and trustworthy. Their word means something, so many complicated problems are solved right then and there when they give it. However, there is a vast difference between the symbols of their differing cultures, which indicates the nature of the cultures themselves, most notably, in the weapons they use in warfare. In the Eastern cultures of Japan, there is a subset of samurai called ninjas who used covert stealth and irregular combat to achieve their tactical objectives. Then in the West, the gunfighter used skill and force to make their point and eliminate a barrier. The difference couldn't be more obvious, yet from the East, many modern bounty hunters make their livings using terminology from the ninja culture to inspire the West elements desired for business improvement without adequately understood actual effects.

In the East, it's all about melee combat, hand-to-hand fighting, and the use of swords. Primarily gunpowder wasn't developed as part of their warfare culture because there was always some emperor wanting to stay in power, whether we are talking about China, Japan, the Koreas, or Southeast Asia wrapping around the world over into India. The ability to defend yourself from other unarmed warriors was revered, but the goal was never to protect private property but rather a territorial lord of some kind. This mentality was quickly transferred over into modern times, where a corporation replaced the lord. There the skills of the ninja or the more direct samurai warrior found a home. Instead of protecting the house of their lord with a sword, they turned that ambition to their employer. Since as an evolutionary society, the emphasis was to sacrifice their lives for their lords. The gun development in their cultures was never matured, leaving the value of their antics to emphasize precision over effectiveness as the individual contributors were considered secondary to the gains made. Since the individuals involved in the warfare were deemed expendable as they always are in collective-based societies, the ultimate weapons of effectiveness and preservation were never unleashed.

However, in the West, starting in Europe and being the tour de force of all movement into America was this idea of personal gain and the acquisition of wealth without the endorsement of a regional governor or a king's court. Since reliance on the state was not required to obtain riches and land, weapons more conducive to individual preservation were needed, so the art of gunfighting developed along those lines of thinking. With the improvement of the gun, individuals didn't need an army to protect their lands and possessions from vile undesirables. They only required plenty of ammunition and a basic understanding of how to shoot a gun. A ball and musket allowed great frontiersmen like Simon Kenton and Daniel Boone to tame the wild frontier. Oh, and let's never forget Simon Girty! While the Indians needed to get gunpowder and ammunition from trade, the young Americans could make their own, giving them the jump to claim the gains they made and bring Western culture to the East, settling the bet before it was even made.

To this day, the effectiveness of the ninja arts and the samurai are used in business for many reasons. The company itself becomes a kind of "mini-state" where the governments tend to be very authoritarian. The company's gains preside over the individuals who are expected to sacrifice themselves for the greater good. In that relationship, the state isn't willing to give individuals the ability to do for themselves so much as they are expected to protect the state itself with their very life. This is the cause of many companies embracing wise concepts of the East because it was a similar kind of thinking from which they were already committed. However, the results are predictable and just as unambitious. For the bounty hunters searching for a method that will bring sustainability to a company, either large or small, these East ways made sense. If a company just wanted to exist and only needed occasional sacrifices by their warriors to succeed, then the teaching of the samurai and ninja were acceptable. Instead of the ancient ways of combat emphasizing permanent gains acquired, such as the West's methods, the nature of competitive warfare became the way to have the mindset of battle without the warriors migrating over to personal gains.

Hand-to-hand fighting, however, is a young person's game. As you get older, you don't feel like jumping all over the place trying to kick your opponent in the face or get close to them to break their arms and legs. In Western culture, we just shoot them and move on with our lives. If whoever we hit threatened our sanctity with deadly force, the case is clear, which is the nature of all things in Western culture. In the West, it was discovered that we didn't want to get close to our enemies, nor was there honor in hand-to-hand combat. The closest we came to such an act in the West was boxing and knife fighting, which never really took hold the way a gunfighter's duel did. The fights of the gunfighter were about more than just killing the other person; they were in defense of the ultimate prize, the preservation of individualized private property. So while in the East, the emphasis was on finding ways to punch harder to be more efficient and productive while in combat, in the West, it was about building bigger guns, where the mechanics of the fight were placed into the hands of technology. Guns made individuals much more powerful and could then fight off a whole army of ninjas, throwing their sticks and metal stars.

That same mentality is just as effective in modern business; the emphasis on skills directly translates over to the effectiveness of a business endeavor. While precision and effectiveness of combat study in service to the state can yield good results, nothing is ever more explosive than when a business can align itself with the personal desires and push for wealth that comes from the individuals who make up the business. When the needs of individuals are aligned with the requirements of a business, great things can happen, which is the difference between the gunfighter and the ninja, or the Wild West sheriff or the samurai warrior protecting their feudal lords. Microsoft in the West was very successful in just the same kind of way initially, as was Apple. Many of their employees became very wealthy as the gains of a new type of gold rush were positioned for the taking. Information technology became the new panning for gold, and no place else on earth competed. As a result, to compete against those two companies, the needs of the business were aligned to match the needs of individuals who wanted to do good work and get wealthy in the process. The results are unmistakable. While the argument can be made that gunfighter speed and accuracy are attached directly, the mechanics of a gun and its bullets are more effective than raw precision. The samurai sword became and remained a symbol. A firearm is the best weapon for fulfilling individual needs in business and life, and when individual needs are aligned with a business, explosive results occur.

CHAPTER NOTES:

a. It is not about which is better, the East or the West; it's about philosophy and the goals of an endeavor.
b. In the East, there are the ninjas who used melee combat and precision to their strategic goals. In the West, the gunfighters and the innovation and brute force of abundance carried the day.
c. The samurai focused on protecting the house of their lord. The gunfighter used their guns for personal gain without the endorsement of a king's court.
d. Individuals in the West didn't need an army to protect their lives, they had their guns, and growth was decentralized.

THE VICO CYCLE AND THE GUN

In the West, the powerful gun and the inventions of precise and complicated mechanics were emphasized, not the hand-to-hand precision of combat in close quarters. The invention itself equalizes the matter with the gun, not the skill one acquires after many hours of practice to get close to an opponent and render them dominated by desire. Just to think of the American Indian who had been for centuries using chipped rocks tied to the end of carved sticks to do most of their hunting and acts of aggression. Then along comes a different version of humanity with devices that shoot metal projectiles from a safe distance, and there just wasn't any way to stop them. That same mentality can be said to permeate the central issue between Western and Eastern manufacturing techniques. It may be second nature to turn inward on a problem and find a way to turn the individual into an instrument for the group, to be a better hunter or warrior to protect the greater good. In the West, the issue is often settled well before the other party can even react due to the nature and mechanics of a typical firearm in comparison.

In business, just as in all other aspects of life, there are cycles of success and regression best explained by the Vico Cycle, a series of events that seem always to predicate each other only to return to their origins predictably. The Vico Cycle is an intellectual contribution of Giambattista Vico contemplated during the golden age of piracy from Italy then captured in European literature by the excellent book *Finnigan's Wake*. It was not that reading material was a priority for the early gunfighters two hundred years after the fact; it was the invention of the gun that has broken that eternal cycle for what appears to be the first time in all recorded history. The Vico Cycle states that all cultures and the people within them emerge into the confines of theocracy, then enlighten themselves with education into aristocracy, where the values of individuals are assimilated into an outward social projection. Then comes the democratization of social assets for the general common good as defined by the masses. The cycle ends once the group's order falls into aspects of anarchy only to find redemption back at the beginning with theocracy, turning to the salvation of otherworldly assistance and prayer.

On the level of macro analysis, the Vico Cycle is applied to the rise and fall of nations where each, over time, has had a culture that deemed it superior only to retreat into chaos and hope. Yet on the micro, the business cycles of any commercial enterprise follow the same basic trajectory of thought; a company comes forth with hopes of bringing a product to market. A management system is put in place that uses social order to establish the practices of the group conglomeration. Then it all seems to fall apart; whether we are talking about the car industry or farming, the Vico Cycle has shown that all cycles ebb and flow from success to failure almost as rhythmically as the ocean tide emerges then wanes.

Until the invention of gun powder and the gradual increase of the reliability of the various guns that came to market, the Vico Cycle dominated all aspects of human development. The gun brought stability and state-driven governments of the East to provide a superior culture that emerged where individuals would always put the organization of their employment above their desires. To improve their effectiveness, the individual would then become a weapon sharpened for the needs of the many in the forms of melee combat. Yet once the members of Western culture found that guns in the form first of a ball of metal propelled by black powder could control entire cities such as Blackbeard's siege of Charleston, the power of the individual became much more authoritative. They unleashed a new age of invention due to the promise of vast sums of wealth waiting to be exploited. Quickly guns evolved from crude and inaccurate weapons to rather precise and complicated instruments of Western Expansion. The Vico Cycle was broken in America through that invention, and society was born somewhere between aristocracy and democracy. A new way of conducting business emerged, and it was the gun that made it happen.

Those same forces are very much prevalent in the modern age of business. The Western businessperson is self-empowered to shape their destiny for themselves and the companies they represent. Whereas still in the East, it is all about sacrifice to the organization and close-quarters combat. In the East, precision and hand-to-hand combat were the values because they had to be. In contrast, it was about force and overpowering opposition that ruled the day in the West when it came to the sheer power of mass, such as in the battles of the Alamo or Custer's famous battle of Little Big Horn the domination of groups still won. But to a much less impact as weapons improved and the individuals in possession of them were able to stave off multitudes of insurgents, leaving, in general, the Indians unable to compete. This eventually would be the same type of approach later in World War II, where military actions in Japan and China could not compete against the industrialization of America. Manufacturing in the West was increasingly mechanized, just as the gun had become. From that gun culture, and were used not with an emphasis on precision but on mass themselves. In the East, the individual worked as an element of precision to serve their groups. Still, in the West, the precision of machinery contained the precision and allowed the individuals to fend for themselves. In that fashion, the Wild West had every home erected on the vast plains of what had been Indian territory, its army not requiring group coordination to embark on military victories.

It is that same mentality that exists today in business and how the two cultures approach the topic. For the gunfighter, the precision is not in their application of closed-quarters combat; it is their ability to use a precision weapon toward their desired goals. Rather than get close to their opponent, they'd instead shoot from a distance. In the East, closed quarter combat group directed was the method of advancement for centuries. The American businessperson approaches many of their problems most naturally from a distance. Using mechanized solutions and the power of their success is most notably by their decentralization of thinking. Hand-to-hand combat with melee weapons requires mass to be effective; working in the group context, a decentralized Western approach can gain more ground quicker and from a greater distance.

In this way, the weapons of culture can say a lot about how they conduct business or how successful they will be. And in that context, the American gunfighter certainly has the advantage.

CHAPTER NOTES:

a. The invention of the gun brought to the history of the world a break from the Vico Cycle for the first time.
b. A Vico Cycle is a process for which all civilization starts with a theocracy, aristocracy, democracy, and anarchy. Then back to the beginning over and over again all through time.
c. Once the gun and invention of gunpowder freed individual empowerment, the old order of the power of cultures became irrelevant.
d. The western businessperson is self-empowered and driven for opportunities of profit. In the East, the goal is a sacrifice to the organization, and eventually, the state. The two have very different motivations.

THE MERITS OF DUELING

The concept of getting "satisfaction" from a personal insult went a long way to establishing honor and proper conduct among business transactions in the time before modern rules as we know them today. As we have seen often where various religions and their value are not unified, and therefore cannot be expected to hold up in a court of law, there needs to be a mechanism that brings about honor and holds it into the context of moral conduct. Otherwise, villainy will quickly grow like a weed in a garden of dreams. Dueling in the classic sense, especially in the New World during the American Revolution, answered this problem. If there was an argument against the American Constitution for change, it was in the original rules of the nation that mechanisms of honor were established before the courts were needed.

In doing business in the Orient, particularly in Japan, where honor is still an admirable trait, business transactions are accelerated because the interactions mean something with one another. Honor is evident at the airports around Tokyo among men and women as respect is a universal language that makes interactions between people start on common ground. In the West, we have allowed our own culture of respect to drift away into the more centralized regulation of the state, which outlawed the practice of dueling essentially so that lawyers could profit off the installation of justice. The cost was that individual satisfaction for an insult did not respect what it deserved. The emphasis was on protecting society from itself by settling matters in a court of law. Legal deferment has led our culture to adapt to a more passive-aggressive society where trust isn't always easy to find in other people. It could be argued that we were all better off when we tried to openly kill each other to protect a slight against our names.

Dueling was so common at the start of America that the governor of South Carolina wrote a book on it to make sure everyone did it right called *The Code of Honor: Or Rules for the Government of Principals and Seconds in the Art of Dueling* in 1834 by John Lyde Wilson. Dueling in the time of the Revolutionary War was quite common. It was slowly going out of style at the start of our republic form of the government to phase disputes into what many considered a more civilized way. In the South, particularly in Charleston, South Carolina, dueling was so common that the governor felt compelled to create legal means of settling disputes. It might sound barbaric compared to our modern legal system, but hindsight seemed to generate more responsible people on an individual level. Protecting honor certainly helped in business commerce because if a business deal went wrong, the parties might find themselves in the streets fighting to the death to obtain their satisfaction.

The critical aspect of satisfaction is that the emphasis was on the individual reputations of the participants. It wasn't some third-party "state" that decided justice, it was the people at the heart of the conflict, and in many ways, society was more honorable. People had to treat each other individually better as a result. The more the states intruded on managing people's affairs, the more passive-aggressive disputes have become, leaving business conduct to suffer greatly. After the Civil War, it was particularly immigrants from the South who moved West searching for gold and other opportunities. They took with them the concept of dueling that had been very much a part of early American life. Dueling with fast draw had a way of bringing honor where there wasn't yet law and forced people to treat each other better and more honorably, which is why there is still reverence for it.

At the state level, we can all see today that the concept of taking honor and responsibility for good conduct away from individuals has been a mistake. While dueling was a violent concept, the number of people who died from it was arguably much less frequent than the kind of violence we see today. Thinking like a gunfighter is better than the modern context of settling disputes. There is enough history to see the flaws by those not directly responsible for the conduct. Instead of getting satisfaction for an honor tainted, we say "see you in court" instead of settling the matter right then and there. Then, of course, those who can pay for the best lawyer become the winners in most cases, and the state enjoys the revenue and job opportunities that come from settling disputes. But what is lost is the individual responsibility for the actions taken and the merit of an honorable exchange. Taking the example of the famous duel between General Gladsten and General Howe in 1778, both Generals in the Revolution were in dispute over troop possession. They took to the streets of Charleston, South Carolina, where many such duels were taking place at the time, and when the time came, they stared each other down, waiting for the other to make a move. After taunting each other for a good bit of time, finally, General Howe fired his pistol and clipped the ear of Gladsten. Gladsten, in response, who was thought to be the John Adams of the South and inventor of the famous "Don't Tread on Me" flag, deliberately fired his shot into the ground, inviting Howe to try again. Eventually, the two men shook hands, settling their dispute with only a minor injury occurring to Gladsten's ear. Otherwise, the business between two prominent Revolutionary War figures was agreed upon respectfully, something that indeed wouldn't have happened if the two had fought it out in court with lawyers acting as their pistols and fancy words spoken in legal jargon as bullets.

The matter is not that dueling is a desired trait or that we should bring it back in its form. Killing another person isn't a desirable outcome for any dispute. Still, the finality of it tended to put in the participant's minds the seriousness of an issue. This mindset certainly set the West and its expansion ablaze with an activity that any legal system couldn't have regulated at the rate that human ambition was expanding at the time. The potential preserved the honor for dueling, and this threat allowed for proper respect when a nation needed it most. We could learn a lot from then to apply today where integrity among business transactions desperately lacks respect, particularly within the American borders. Other countries have honor-driven rituals, and it is noticeable during business transactions. In the United States, however, we have allowed our laws to be governed by lawyers and judges who take away the responsibility for personal conduct. They then place it in the hands of the state, and many of our businesses have followed. The impact has been a loss in honor among business interactions that have not been desirable. Yet integrity could be restored if only we stepped back into hindsight and dusted off the values that emerged from dueling and upgraded that sentiment for our modern needs, which starts by thinking like a gunfighter.

CHAPTER NOTES:

a. Getting satisfaction from a personal insult has shaped much of the way we do business today.
b. Dueling originally established mechanisms of honor before the courts became involved.
c. Losing the ability to duel and replacing that practice with the court of law where lawyers became the weapons and courts our bullets have left us with a less trustworthy society.
d. The government initially saw the need for dueling to preserve honor among populations. Without honor, transactions between people have greatly diminished.

WAR

In many ways, business is like war, and the rules of conduct are very similar. War in every circumstance is about depleting your enemy while outlasting them to some capitulation. When we fight on the playground as youths, one of the first hard lessons that we must learn is not what it feels like to put a fist against the flesh of another person, which is an odd sensation, but in how we can know who won. Not what we see in the movies. It's how to win those fights so that later when both sides are declaring a victory just for showing up, the world can know who won. The winner is the one who must yield to the other who is ready to capitulate. As many often are, the fight can be small and intimate; they can be in an MMA fight in front of people or between companies fighting for market share. Ultimately, they may be between countries. Fighting and war, in general, is about making the other side lose, in desiring to no longer fight. That is the name of the game, and for the gunfighter, often in the great games of chess that are always going on in business and politics, they are the great knights and bishops who can move well around the board, striking at their opponents quickly and effectively.

Wars are won with mass and efficiency. Just like the schoolyard fights that are still quite common, even if the rivalries have moved into online gaming more than actual fists to faces, the punches come fast and furious in the opening moments. But within 30 seconds of such a fight, the burn in your lungs takes over, and there is usually a slight panic at how tired you are. Adrenaline begins to wear off, and that is where doubt comes into play. The path to losing is not far behind, and winners know how to go in for the kill. These fights are often wars of duration, but their patterns are no different from the intimate personal conflicts of one-on-one combat. Big companies may be going after the same military contract, and they are fighting for market share in precisely the same way. That kind of fighting is considered good and healthy for capitalist endeavors. So long as politics stay out of the process, the best often win, giving the market superior products due to the competition.

Using the Charleston example again, since so much of what became part of the Old West emerged from the areas of South Carolina after the Civil War, it was the war between North and South that ultimately serves as the best mode of understanding war and its necessity. The attack on Fort Sumter by the South against a North garrison stationed there to keep the unruly southerners under control occurred a month after the inauguration of the great president Abraham Lincoln. That election alone let the South know that lifestyle choices in the future were not going to go their way, so they decided to leave the Union and attack the troops stationed at Sumter. Visiting Fort Sumter today, which should be a requirement of all Americans and their educations, the situation is obvious. The battle was fought for blood and killing as many people as possible on both sides. The goal was to let the other government know that if the war continued that soon there wouldn't be any more troops left to play with. Eventually, one side or the other would run out of resources and the will to win.

At the start, the will to win was clearly on the side of the South, and for the first few years of the war, it looked like the South would win. President Lincoln knew how to play the long game, like any tremendous individual fighter who wears out their opponent by sticking close to the ropes until oxygen is starved in their rivals. The rivals scream silently for an end of the conflict because they can't keep up the fighting pace forever, and they know it. In the end, the South just ran out of resources. They may have had all the will to fight and to spread the menace of war from ocean to ocean. Still, in the end, it was the sheer will and dominance of the industrial North that cut through the South and allowed Sherman to be on the high side of negotiations forcing Savannah and Charleston to pick between destruction or to save their cities with capitulation. In both cases, the residents there knew what had happened to Columbia and Atlanta, and they didn't want to see the same happen to them, so they surrendered their cities to allow their excellent work to at least continue. And that is how you win against an enemy in all cases, micro and macro. Make them choose while staying on the high side of the process.

Many of those Southern fighters weren't ready to capitulate and felt that their government had let them down, so they moved West searching for a new life, giving rise to the many stories of Wild West adventures that we hear about today. The Civil War continued for another twenty to thirty years, not ending until electricity brought civilization to the far corners of North America. But in those cases, the great gunfighters who had been rooks and bishops in the great war were without a chessboard, and their fights were misdirected and resentful, not focused and strategic, which is ultimately why they lost. Like in the case of all battles, personal, corporate, or political, knowing what defines a win and sticking with it is what matters. The winner is always the one who makes the other surrender. The fight cannot allow both sides just to walk away and declare themselves as winners to their friends and partners. The definition of victory must be followed until the other party surrenders to save their face from destruction or preserve their reputations to fight another day. But the conquest of the other is necessary, and in business, that is the way of it. Just because business suits and emails have replaced guns and cannons, the concept is the same. It's not just about killing off all the resources of the other party; it's about making them not want to fight any longer. While the gunfighter is part of the strategy of making others want to surrender, the overall objective is that your side wins and that everyone understands that is the name of the game.

The goal in anything is not that everyone gets a trophy or is friendly to each other. The purpose of all conflict is to bring about the best and let the world ride off the efforts of those defined victories. If you cannot define a victory, you can be said not to win or lose. The purpose of playing every game that we have as a civilization is to teach our youth how to win and how not to lose. However, once the games are over, real-life demands action, and the battles must commence, whether you are ready for them. War and conflict are part of human life, and they are needed to bring forth the best ideas and establish them as a future state, as in the future belongs to the victors. If you want to let the enemy live in harmony after the winner is declared, that is up to you. But you must always look to destroy the other side so that they lose their will to fight. Especially concerning business, because that is the way things are in life.

CHAPTER NOTES:

a. War in every circumstance is about forcing the other party to capitulate. The winner is the one who pushes the other to surrender. To make them no longer want to fight.
b. So long as politics stay out of the way, the best usually wins, and a free market brings about the justice of competing parties.
c. In the Civil War, the South started with the will to win, but Lincoln and his strategy robbed that will until a clear winner was obvious eventually.
d. The losing South moved West to begin again, and the wars were more individualized than institutional, which gave birth to the American Gunfighter. Business suits and emails have replaced the guns, but the game has not changed. All conflict aims to define the best of a culture and establish a future state of victory.

MONEY IS NOT THE ROOT OF ALL EVIL; IT REVEALS IT

There are still many who didn't want the concept of America ever to become a reality. The people most guilty of this concept proclaim that money is the root of all evil, one of the most ridiculous notions ever evoked. Money is, in all honesty, the most moral measure of value, and it is why the American system became the most honest on planet earth, not just in opinion but in the measured value. It all started with Adam Smith's excellent book, *The Wealth of Nations,* printed in 1775 and culminated with the Wild West gunfighters of the post-Civil War period. For the first time, the definitions of freedom and justice were established. People of all skin types and backgrounds could make their way in the world and have access to wealth in whatever quantities it could be generated, whether during the gold rush, playing cards in saloons, or through the upcoming railroads and farming that erupted along those lines. Adam Smith discovered the concept of the "invisible hand," and through it established a new kind of governing with a Bill of Rights; it was the gun that protected that hand, which gave way to massive amounts of undiscovered wealth.

Before this time, it was always kingdoms who divided up the spoils of economics and distributed them among their courts and acquisitions. To become well off in this kind of culture, you had to be well connected. When Western Expansion happened in America, many of those voices were very jealous to lose their power. They hated the new Bill of Rights and the guns that protected them so that the "invisible hand" of economics could take flight. Of course, we can see this invisible hand at work when taking a trip down the highway at 3 AM, where we wonder where all those people are going and at all random times. In business, we count on that invisible hand to bring the revenue we operate off of. If our business is a restaurant along a highway, it's different people who come to us every day, but they come in patterns born out of necessity. It's our job to discover that necessity, and for those who do, they can expect to become rich in the process. So how could anybody point to money and say that it is the root of all evil?

Well, many would point to the stagecoach robbers and those who hijacked the first trains traversing the country and say that the lure of money collected in those places brought out the evil of humanity. However, this would be incorrect; it was the collection of money that showed the actual value of the people themselves. Where there is money, there is always an honest appraisal of the morality of humanity. Money is generated through productivity, people who work and do things. That is how it is made. Then how that money flows through society brings about the truth of what moral conduct people behave. In times prior the ethical conduct was often hidden behind the political movements of those times, but in this new America on the wild frontier, honest people and dishonest people were pushed into the light of day due to the nature of money. Of course, some did the work of taming the West and worked at "making money." Then some sought to take money from others in poker and robbing stagecoaches, hoping to get a lot of money without doing the labor of earning it, and we have always thought of those people as evil or lacking morality.

To bring about the fundamental nature of people, money needs to exist. Otherwise, the villains always hoard the resources that society needs in their castles and bloodlines. The question has never been that money was the root of all evil; it was in that it brought about the true nature of evil, those who didn't want to work to make it, and those who were willing to invent new ways of generating it through labor and ingenuity. Also, it was the gun that stood between the two and the gunfighter who defined justice. The bad were the ones stealing the wealth created by the good. Even in our modern times, it is the private ownership of guns that protects wealth and keeps bad people from barging in on every tiny home that might hold some treasure to rob. The creation of wealth itself is not evil. However, it is evil to want to shortcut its earning, making it or stealing it. Without money, there isn't a proper definition for evil to regulate conduct. And when people are willing to steal money by breaking the law, there isn't any law that a politician can come up with to stop them. Only a gunfighter standing on the side of good and justice can. That holds today.

For anybody in business, they understand this paradox well; all businesses are there to make money. If the saying about money being the root of all evil is true, isn't every company evil, and then our participation in their conduct? But alas, it is the opposite that is true. It is good to work in a business and to help it make money lots of money. Money is the very definition of morality; its creation makes greatness and reveals the heart of the good, the bad, and the treacherous. The hearts of all people are then shown to be because money makes the definitions obvious. Whether the morality of money is shown in the boisterous overconsumption of those who want to show others how much they have, or whether it is the plotter who would instead steal the money than earn it, it is the making of money that establishes morality. The businesses that make the most can be the most significant contributors to morality on planet earth.

However, wherever money is made, protections are needed. That is where the mind of the gunfighter comes into play. Without the gun, Adam Smith's invisible hand would have never seen the light of day. Once every home in the rapidly expanding America had access to a gun, then the value of money had some protection that was not centralized. Guns allowed money to be made in the far reaches of Nevada and California during the gold rush without an army garrison there to protect its production. Who needed such a thing when everyone had a gun? That is why owning and using guns contributes significantly to society's morality and why making money will always be protected by the gunfighter. The great gunfighters of the world preserve the making of money from those who would otherwise steal it, which then accurately shows the character of our human population. No such device could ever really be considered evil. Instead, the evil is in not knowing or having a mechanism that brings villainy into the light of day.

CHAPTER NOTES:

a. Many never wanted the concept of America to be developed because of the economic pressure that was applied to the world under Adam Smith's ideas. The individualized use of the gun protected the concept of the invisible hand.
b. Money shows the value of humanity itself. Money is made through productivity and therefore reveals the character of the people who make it.
c. When money is made without being attached to productivity, we can easily see the villains of society through this method.
d. Without money, there isn't a proper definition for the value of a society to be measured. Money is the very definition of morality.

THE NATURE OF WORKPLACE POWER

Every business must put up with the gradual corruption of leadership utilizing their acquired power. It is difficult for many people to resist the power of managing other people's affairs; it is easy for them to get lost in all the restricted potential of their own lives and live out those ambitions through others without the risk themselves. That is often the very foundation of corruption, and it is as common as raindrops in a storm. All businesses find themselves having to contend with this actual state of human relationships, the power players. Ironically the same traits that make great leaders also take people perilously close to the degradation of the power players, so it is nearly impossible to avoid. In the times of the Wild West, this kind of thing happened all the time; the good sheriff would find themselves on the wrong side of robberies and murders. Then again were the criminals who wanted to make a clean break for justice. There were very few truly good people like Bass Reeves from the Oklahoma territory.

Bass Reeves was an interesting case; he was the first black U.S. Marshal west of the Mississippi River and was credited over his career for over 3000 arrests across the Arkansas and Oklahoma territories, including his son. The latter had killed the man his wife was having an affair with. As a gunfighter, he killed at least 14 people in self-defense. It was likely that the legends of Bass Reeves spilled out of prison in Detroit into the radio studio nearby as the Legend of the Lone Ranger was born. From the many incidents of heroics initiated from the inmate's banter trickling out into the outside world, truth spilled over into fantasy, and a cinematic hero was born. It was hard only a few decades after the Civil War to admit to themselves that a black man had been such a noble and heroic figure in the Old West. Hence, filmmakers took liberties with the appearance of the Lone Ranger. Still, the essence of the real person was unmistakably good, which are precisely the same traits needed for those who ultimately have the power of justice in their possession.

For Bass Reeves, he was a person beyond corruption, and every element of his existence breathed for a sense of justice for all, even when it cost him personally. That is the kind of person that we all want in our businesses managing our human resources. However, once the power over others is given, we don't find a Bass Reeves, but a cold, dark villain who will use the power of their badge to harm those under them. And under those kinds of conditions, that is where the gunfighters are needed. For in the stories of the Old West, when such corruption happened, a shootout would ensue, and the corrupt person might survive a few challenges, but eventually, they'd be killed. That is not the case in our modern world, where such shootouts are illegal. Though there are other ways to challenge oppressors, the time is ripe for such an exchange when those oppressors appear.

A good manager should be like Bass Reeves, completely incorruptible and honest about everything they do. Their sole intent should be justice for all and the sustainability of their employer. In their eyes, justice should be truly blind even when their friends and family are the perpetrators of evil. Evil in this definition is the one established in this book, those who are good are those who seek to make money with labor and productivity. Evil is those who seek to acquire money without earning it. The good manager is the one who stands by the side of good, the productive, the hard-working, and the honest clock puncher who seeks to do everything right by way of the company they work for. The evil is those looking to get through the day doing as little as possible and hide their efforts behind the antics of chaos. They come back from a break too late; they are constantly pushing back against productive requirements. They seek to make others into bad people so that they are not alone in their efforts. These are the conditions that a good manager must guard against.

However, it is all too easy to side with the bad because it is hard to be good. So, as the manager, if they do not support the good, they feed the bad, and soon there will be many more inclined to evil because justice was not embraced. People looking out for their well-being will side with whatever force is winning in a workplace. That is why all managers must seek to be like Bass Reeves and stand for truth, justice, and honor with every breath they take. Good management is not something that anybody can fake. It would help if you stood by those traits all hours of the day, all days of the week, even when nobody is looking.

When the management of a business embraces good practices, then the products will reflect the effort, and a definite competitive edge will be evident to all. That is the way to success. However, power corrupts because it often goes unchallenged, and great evil will spread over the entire organization. Unlike the days of the past when evil percolated into the lives of the innocent, we cannot take those people out into the street and shoot them dead. We must outwit them and out manage them, but we must attack them, nonetheless. The more logical path of engaging villainy at gunpoint may be more complicated today than it was yesterday. Still, the efforts of the good manager standing on the side of justice are just as needed as it was in Bass Reeves' time on the wild frontier.

We all know examples of putting a badge of honor on what we think of as good people who immediately let the power go to their heads, and they become destructive. They start to seek shortcuts in life using their ability to get them access, whether it is a designated parking spot or a free lunch at some restaurant where the owners trade a meal to access the power the abuser possesses. But the best of us in every business should be on the lookout for the modern examples of Bass Reeves, who only knows justice and wouldn't trade that understanding for all the gold and riches placed at their feet. In that way, they are beyond corruption and cannot be bought with luxury or temptations of an easy life. They live as examples of a higher order, and those under their command are happy to follow them to the ends of the earth because they know they can be trusted under any circumstance. Once such a person is given power in any place of business, it is assured success will come into that industry; for such a person to exist is so rare. That is why all companies should be on the lookout for such people, and when they see them, to care for them. They stand between good and evil, success and failure, and the very concept of justice, whether on the wild frontier or in the cubicles of industry. People have and will always be people. Great leaders are like the great gunfighter and law officer Bass Reeves, far more significant than Hollywood legends could fathom. There are more of them out there. It is the business task of the industry to find them and put them to work in all the good ways that all companies need.

CHAPTER NOTES:

a. It is challenging to regulate the temptations that come from managing the affairs of subordinates. The creation of the power players creates a lot of misery.
b. Bass Reeves was a Texas sheriff who was truly good and never abused his power. As a black man, he had one of the best records as a person of the law and never became corrupted by his power over others.
c. A good manager should be like Bass Reeves; justice should always be blind. Evil people are those looking to make money without earning it. The good are those who create value through productivity. The good manager must always guard the good against the bad without losing focus on justice.
d. Power corrupts because it often goes unchecked. After all, there are not enough good people to stand for justice.

THE PARASITIC MICROMANAGER

Overmanaging is a real problem for most organizations, where leadership feels it must micromanage every little thing. Micromanaging is a terrible trait and always leads to failure. Ultimately this trait is directly connected to our culture and the types of warfare we utilized in the past and favor this very day. Going back to the primitive days of the civilizations that had not yet learned to use gunpowder as a means of obtaining food and defending themselves, the knife or a bow and arrow made society much less efficient. It may have been quite rewarding to hunt an animal with such devices. Still, ultimately when firearms were invented to utilize the power of gun powder, the next generation of mass management had come to be and essentially is the key to all industrialization in our modern times.

For the micromanager in every business, the primary disfunction of their volition is that they aren't using the tools around them to perform the targeted task. For instance, if the goal is to hit a bullseye on a target, that objective could be hit with an arrow or a bullet. If the defined plan is to hit the target, then either way of doing so could be effective. But suppose we further determined the parameters by saying that we need to hit the target fast or repeatably. In that case, it will quickly become evident that the bow and arrow just isn't the most efficient tool to perform the objective. It might be the individually more rewarding, but not the conducive method of achieving a goal.

The micromanager is doing everything wrong because essentially, they insist on keeping the goals achieved within the realm of their limits which is like saying that we will only hit targets within the restrictions of using a bow and arrow. Some archers may become quite good at such a task, but ultimately, they will fail compared to the mechanization of a gun when the objectives of the targets are considered equal. The micromanager instead restricts the flow of effort by their limits. Thinking in terms of East meets West or the cowboy and the Indian, when conflict ensues between two cultures, utilizing optimization and micromanaging, the optimization will win every time.

It takes great effort to shoot an arrow from a bow to hit a target. There is a lot of manual operation to perform the task, let alone repeatedly get the same results. At the same time, a gun is a precision machine with lots of tightly measured tolerances built into the device to allow the user to point and shoot the same way every time. The velocity and power come from the gun powder. The aiming and other alignments come from the mechanics themselves. Whereas the bow and arrow require all the aiming and velocity to be instigated by the shooter, their time and energy are much less effective in sustained battle.

A good shooter with a gun is like a sound manager; they trust the mechanisms within the gun to do their specific jobs. All they need to worry about is aiming and firing. The chambering of a bullet, the power behind the shot, and the pull of the trigger that releases the hammer are not even considerations that the shooter thinks about. Their task in maintaining those items is in the care of the firearm itself; it's oiling and cleaning. But when it comes time to shoot, the good shooter, like the good manager, trusts the weapon and all its functions to do their jobs, leaving them to focus their energy on sending the bullet where it needs to go.

In business, this is comparable to the sales department hitting their targets for margins and delivery. They need to trust all the mechanisms that deliver the objective, the parts of the organization that load the quote, make the product, and deliver it on time to the customer. They need to trust that the organization can hit what they are aiming at and that their function is to make sure the targets get hit. They don't want to go into all their supporting departments and micromanage all those efforts toward an objective because in doing so, they would not enjoy the gains that their modern method of doing things affords them. Even a lousy gun well-worn that occasionally misfires is better in a battle over a bow and arrow. So even in a bad performance, a gun is better than other melee weapons in winning battles, just as trusting the mechanics of an organization will consistently outperform the micromanager. If there was ever an important lesson to learn during Western Expansion, guns beat knives, bows, arrows, and spears every time, so long as there were ammunition and guns to shoot them with. There may be nobility in having the ability to do every part of the task in shooting, but the effectiveness needs to come from the weapons themselves, and the shooter needs to trust those mechanics.

In this fashion, it is the reason that the gunfighter of the Old West was and continues to be the most effective warrior the world has ever seen. While other cultures were experts in the melee operations of weapons and could be quite deadly in hand-to-hand combat, ultimately, the gun allowed for the expansion of effort through the trust of the mechanics, which took the burden of force and effort away from the shooter. In every business, most departments' sole function is to be parts of a gun that the good manager aims in the correct direction to hit the objective, not just once, but repeatedly with the same effectiveness. While the six-shooters entered the world of the Indian, the primitive weapons that allowed for the hunt of deer and buffalo for centuries were no match because the six-shooter, with all its precision mechanics, allowed the gunfighter to use those tools to their most significant effect.

While the micromanager wants to show the world what great warriors they are, that they can string a bow or pull an arrow from the quiver on the back of a horse and shoot during a gallop, the micromanager is easily beaten by the user of a six-shooter who knows that the gun itself is an organization of precision that they can trust. They need to worry about hitting their target; it's not the process we should be concerned with; it's the results. The old world might bellyache about this excessive effectiveness provided by the gun, but the results are unmistakable. And it is so that every organization that is thinking like a gunfighter instead of a primitive hunter can expect to be very successful. The trick is in trusting the mechanics of your organization so that the effort can utilize effectiveness. Being a good warrior isn't nearly as important as being on the winning side of a war. So, with that definition, the gunfighter is the most effective warrior globally, not because their war skills are better, but are instead better utilized.

CHAPTER NOTES:

a. Overmanaging is a real problem for most organizations, which ultimately leads to failure.
b. Micromanagers in every business share the primary disfunction of their volition because they do not use the tools available to them. They insist on tools they understand within their limits of conceptualization.
c. A good shooter with a gun is like a sound manager; they trust the mechanisms of their concern to do the work sought after.
d. The gunfighter was the most effective warrior globally because they used mechanics to perform their tasks without all the manual concerns of using the weapons themselves. Trusting the mechanics of your organization to better utilization is the key to success.

UNDER COMMITTING AND OVERPERFORMING

These days in business tend to promise to under-commit but over-perform when pressed for schedule improvements and delivery. Undercommitting is a real problem because it doesn't give a business interaction any real value. Since you can't trust what anybody tells you, it's not just a little thing at a few companies; it has become pretty much the standard policy among big and small organizations. They say it is better to look like a hero than overcommit and come out like a villain; that is a deceitful practice that I have personally never gotten used to. Growing up as a kid who watched many Westerns and had grandparents who espoused those values of the honest lawman who told the truth no matter what, this deceitful practice of lying about what could be done is reprehensible. You could look like a hero by pulling rabbits out of your hat at the last minute, but that would be not very honest. Why pretend to be a hero when you can be one?

Many stories of the Wild West gunfighters came from the dandy dime-store novelists who went West searching for fortunes. By writing about the adventures for all those on the East Coast who didn't have the courage or resources to live the untamed life, the gunfighter provided a safe vehicle for conceptualizing courage. Many gunfighters who had killed many people on the frontier fell for the temptation to over-tell their stories for the dandy authors rather than tell what really happened. Inflation of the facts has been the norm in the press during the entire 20th century. If it was one drunken loser outside a saloon in Wyoming on a hot summer night, by the time the dime store novelist was finished with the telling, it was a posse of crazed maniacs and a gunfighter during a vicious nighttime storm complete with a tornado that the hero survived. And from there, many of the great Westerns were told during the early days of cinema.

To me, there has always been dishonesty in this practice. Sure, the bad guys in the stories were still eliminated even if the details were highlighted, and most people just don't see anything wrong with that way of telling a story. So it should not be a surprise that the exact mechanisms have entered into our business practices. It is far easier to look like a hero by setting the expectations low than being a real hero and delivering on time even when there are many excuses not to. The differences in approach come down to sheer laziness and dishonesty. It is hard to set goals more ambitious than reality usually permits and drive everyone to achieve the task, even if the results fall short of what the dime store novelist might write. Usually, when more aggressive goals are set, and people have to chase after them to be a "hero," there is a letdown because usually not everything gets achieved, yet much more happens than if you set the goals low.

The real hero in a place of business isn't necessarily the person getting the award for being a hero by setting targets low and achievable for their cumbersome organization but setting aggressive goals and may not have hit them all but overperforms those who weren't so bold. The reason that few people heard about the Bass Reeves and his 3000 arrests on the plains of the Wild West, but people did hear about a few losers at the OK Corral that Wyatt Earp, Doc Holliday, and the Earp brothers fought in a closed quarter gunfight is that the expectations for Earp were low. In contrast, Reeves was a man of color doing a lawman's job, which nobody else wanted to do. And he was so good at it that nobody wanted to live up to the standard he had set. In contrast, people could relate to Wyatt Earp. He had lost his brothers and outlived everyone involved in the famous shootout in Tombstone. Earp was relatable; he hung out with prostitutes in the brothels, and was a gambler, he was the kind of person that people could understand, so his story was one worth telling. At the same time, Bass Reeves was just too good for most people to understand. Later on, movies were made about the Wild West, and John Wayne was learning how to be a lawman from Wyatt Earp himself on movie sets. Producers made the Lone Ranger into a white guy wearing a mask instead of the real-life black man that

Bass Reeves was in reality. The reason wasn't just to deal with racist sentiments that were still brewing from the end of the Civil War, but because Reeves was just too good, and the writers of those early movies knew that their audience couldn't relate to such people. But the truth about that particular gunfighter was better than the reality performed. Making the Lone Ranger into a guy hiding his identity, at least, was something people understood. The truth about the fearless pursuer of justice that Reeves was couldn't be true for most people.

It is much easier for people to relate to heroics when the context of villainy and the temptation to underperform is what they fight through for a short period of their life to achieve some great event. It is far more challenging to be a hero every day with every breath you take. Such a person doesn't look so great from moment to moment because they are always good. In business, where most of the people you are dealing with are fighting off some temptation toward laziness, it is easier for them to justify themselves with occasional heroics framed under the disguise of under commitments. To promise, five villains shot dead in the street but only killing in reality four and wounding the fifth is setting the bar too high for most. People who don't want to live up to such high standards will always say, "only promise one, and if you kill four, everyone will say you are a hero. But if you say five and only kill four, everyone will be disappointed." In truth, people are disappointed because these heroics are only on display a few times in a year or even a lifetime.

In comparison, the best among us think like Bass Reeves. We make a promise and stick by it, always looking to improve ourselves. If the number is one, four, or twenty, we always try to hit our target, and we do so every day of the year, all years of our lives.

It is better, to be honest, than to be a temporary hero for those who want to keep the expectations for everyone else low by writing about heroes who underperform and even give out rewards to encourage future behavior. In business, everyone needs to understand the reality of a situation. Still, we should not artificially diminish the expectations of the outcome, and we certainly shouldn't lie about what we think we can do so that we can keep the expectations low in the eyes of our partners. To under-commit and over-perform is a lie when the objective is to look like a hero. The real need is for heroes to set aggressive targets and to do everything in their power to hit them, even if those targets appear impossible to average people. Far more will get done that way, especially over time. The definitions of heroics are often defined by people who set low parameters for themselves, so they will not publish the truth because they will not want to live up to those expectations. But to be honest, it is the best way to be a hero and to set aggressive targets for yourself to reach, and that is the way all business conduct should be, always.

CHAPTER NOTES:

a. There is a trend in modern business to under-commit but over-perform to disguise the desire to remove pressure off the performers involved.
b. Under-committing is a deceitful practice built on low ambition, which ultimately shows itself in the quality of the production of everything.
c. It is easy to look like a hero by setting the bar low. But for innovation and the essence of productivity to have justice, the participants need to be pushed to dig deep within themselves to perform a task.
d. It is far more challenging to be a hero every day with every breath you take. Holding back expectations is just another mask for laziness.

THE OPTIMISTIC ART OF WHAT COULD BE

In every business climate, it is essential to understand the terrain of the situation, not just physically or regionally, but intellectually. It is in that examination that the best hints into the advantage of thinking like a gunfighter emerge. This has never been better articulated than in the movement called "Steampunk," an imaginative desire to combine the Victorian Era with the Wild West and a future state technology. The importance of this understanding can't be avoided as it currently touches just about every aspect of human civilization. The Steampunk movement has been a natural outgrowth of optimism created during this period of Wild West expansion, especially in the literary works of Jules Verne and H.G. Wells. As we all look back at the freedoms gained from taming a land with a gun, our imaginations were unleashed by literature from Europe, which migrated through the Victorian culture into the East Coast who would then load up in the trains and head into the newly tamed lands paved by the gunfighters.

It's not that the movement lacks dealing with reality; it's more of a way of understanding how we got where we are and whether we find it acceptable. Globally all of us who call ourselves human are pondering our existence and whether we are ready for the technological innovations that are about to explode upon the scene, many of which will make us feel irrelevant. At the start of the 21st Century, with the big technology firms getting involved in all aspects of living, from politics to primary product consumption, our culture is going back to the beginning of it all, putting together an understanding that will propel us all forward. This is the basic nature of Steampunk. It's also why I say studying the ways of the gunfighter is much more appropriate than any other method of matching the business culture to the needs of civilization. There are many advantages of returning to a time where the Victorian era was coming to an end. Before the Progressive era started, from east to west in the United States, many fascinating perspectives were filling the void behind the violence left in the wake of the Civil War. Things may have happened too fast, so many want to revisit and get things right for the next century.

As the gold rush occurred from the Dakota territories into California, Jules Verne figured out how to launch a rocket from the earth to the moon. He figured out how to get around the world in 80 days. Not all those parts of our culture came together simultaneously, but if they had looked back in hindsight which is always 20/20, we would have had what we now call Steampunk. If your business is in the more technical fields, do not be surprised that your engineers, especially the young ones, are not the same type of people going to cosplay conventions and Steampunk get-togethers. The desire to combine the freedoms of the Old West, the innovations of Einstein, Edison, Tesla, and Verne, and to package it all up into the individual creations of the Victorian era where mass production had not yet taken away the minor tweaks of craftsmanship that found their way into our various products, is desirable. It's especially attractive when considering that our relationship with technology is very much threatening our individuality. If only we could reverse back to the start of the Progressive era, erase our many mistakes, and start over with a much healthier relationship.

Yet we went from the birth of flight just a few years after the Verne novels into landing on the moon just fifty years later. Pulling the world together through air travel did force cultures to interact in ways none of them were comfortable with. If the gunfighter meeting the Indians on the plains of North America was difficult, it was for the East to meet West every day in the world's major airports. Heathrow, which had once been the seat of the British Empire, was now a melting pot of ideas worldwide. Visions were clashing together faster than ever before, and many of us were just hanging on barely for the ride to stop, which it never would. Before we knew it, bounty hunters in the form of consultants were trying to instruct businesses to make money in this rapid state change. Still, due to people's nature and innermost desires, most of the advice came out as worthwhile as a snake oil salesperson pawning whiskey for a miracle tonic.

To understand the people you are working with within a business, it is essential to comprehend Steampunk. Steampunk, that optimistic desire to have all the comforts of technology and its reach into the unlimited depths of space without losing our very souls to the benefits of technology, such as we currently fear with artificial intelligence and information utilization. We want our technology to resemble our hopes and dreams, which was evident in the Victorian era, where that extra bit of craftsmanship was put into the products we made, powered by steam. We don't want to lose ourselves in the technology; we want to see ourselves as it grows and brings forth its bounty. And in all that optimism is a quiet understanding that gunfighting and cutting-edge technology go hand in hand but in some mysterious way, that science and art have not yet been able to put their finger on. Yet, the innate needs of the human being are what they are, and it has splashed on the scene in the form of Steampunk.

It is essential to our topic here because it validates the need to look at our business transactions with the kind of mind that we would during the age of Western Expansion and the morality of the gunfighters of that period. But in that newly created wealth and less centralized governments came the science of Jules Verne. It is the natural state of all people to find in themselves the promise of immortality through technology without losing their sheer essence to the mechanics of mass production. And once that is understood, you can truly understand who you are doing business with and build teams to implement the strategies appropriately. To assume that companies should retreat into the mechanics of Karl Marx, which hit the scene in the mid-1800s and not embrace the optimism of Jules Verne, and all that followed is to ignore the cultural desires of the participants of Steampunk. They want more than anything their individuality captured in the machines we invest in our businesses and make into the reality of our times. They don't want to just be cogs in a machine; they want their individuality to be the machine. Then to get that right, we need to revisit that time when all these elements were coming together rapidly. Perhaps it's not wrong to look at time as an eraser and remove our mistakes, not mistakes made in the wars fought or the bandits killed on dusty streets of new towns erected during the Gold Rush, but in the civilization and centralizing that came during the Progressive era. Once we've done that, we would rebuild businesses with those elements in mind and adapt our management styles to the needs of our employees and the drivers of their hearts that reside truly in their very souls.

CHAPTER NOTES:

a. Steampunk has been a natural outgrowth of Wild West expansion and the art that evolved from the Victorian era, and the opportunities emerging from unleashed imagination.
b. It is attractive to return to a time before the progressive era presented us with an unhealthy relationship with the future.
c. In the time of air travel, the world's visions were clashing together due to a small world suddenly shrinking.
d. We want technology to represent our hopes and dreams; we don't want to lose ourselves in the technology of our times.

A VALUE OF ARTIFICIAL INTELLIGENCE

There is more to the Steampunk movement relevant to modern business as defined by its desire to step over the Progressive era and consider our future state condition with the Victorian era gunfighter in the Wild West. In many ways, Steampunk art is such an unusual combination of past and future. The human desire to create it in the first place is valuable for the emerging businessperson. Increasingly technology has become more a part of all business climates. Technology from the latest computer software does what used to take a room full of people with briefcases to perform. Artificial intelligence will eliminate the need for thousands of employees that certainly won't need to be managed traditionally.

Modifications in technology are the answer to the implications of expanding economies. The human race must outpace the biological reproduction rate. We are going to build cities on Mars, the moon, and places throughout the solar system. We will need more than humans to do all this production work. Even in the best circumstances, we would never keep up as our society migrates into space as a species.

As we manage workers who are increasingly concerned about technology replacing them, it is up to all businesses to reassure them what we know from history, which was very similar to the technology that hit the scene during the end of the 19th century. Christianity was struggling to define itself in that changing climate. Humans as a species struggle with the same considerations even as technology is taking off at a rocket's pace to leave behind all the rules of yesteryear for a frontier not yet discovered. While that can be very exciting, people, in general, fear being left behind. That is why thinking with the courage of a Wild West gunfighter can help bridge emotions from the past into the future—as it had in America before.

The focus on this new age is much like it was, untamed profits unleashed upon the ambitions and innovations of humanity boldly utilized toward an ambitious tomorrow. Only this time, people are more cautious, not in the dangers of expanding technology but losing their individuality, how the Progressive era instigated to close out the 19th century and usher in the 20th. This time people want to make sure that there is a piece of themselves in the technology and that its growth will be a natural extension. So it goes for all of us in business that we must assure our employees and the world of business in general that technology will not replace them but will enhance them. In that way, Steampunk has shown an inclination to help people see themselves in the future.

To go back in time and yearn for something such as the quality of craftsmanship seen in the Victorian era or the freedoms of the Western frontier in North America and to create vast amounts of art about it to assist with understanding the future is not at all an unhealthy attribute. It speaks of a need we all have to pay respect for where we came from and honor it as the future comes quickly into our lives. So far, the idea of technology and artificial intelligence coming from them is sleek and uniform. Most of it was developed from a version of the Progressive era that was very much influenced by written works like *A Brave New World*. But if we have a productive future where everyone has a place in it, then it is up to the business world to shape that destiny with the individualism required to create anything properly.

While most of our future products will shift into new forms of energy, computation, space travel, the idea of medicine, we need to see more of ourselves into the technology of that experience, not in seeing technology just replace the human spirit. It would be my offering that no matter how smart our technology becomes, there will always be advantages to biological machinery in the realm of imagination and abstract concepts that even the best of our mechanical counterparts will always struggle with. And as I have seen much of the Steampunk art displayed in various formats, I see from the effort the desire to fuse imagination with static mathematical equations. The desire to have a grandfather clock instead of a digital alarm clock is a fine example. Both tell time, but one does so with much more outstanding craftsmanship than just a factory-built digital readout.

In their most crude condition, the gunfighter defended the ambitions of humankind without a law formalized to protect all the new businesses that formed along the frontier. Imaginations had to be left to their own devices to produce that expanding economy. That is much what is needed today for managers to protect the ambitions of imagination and reassure everyone that there is a place for them to bring forth future technology. Like the gunfighters of yesteryear, the modern manager must ensure everyone sees the advantage of a future instead of clinging to the past stagnation. Perspective is needed to fill job quotas or leverage a business toward human resources instead of the untapped resources of the oncoming tsunami of imaginative concepts that erupt across our global economy in such exciting ways.

The gunfighter must protect the ambitions of wealth acquisition while promoting life in its essence, biological and invented. Those two aspects need to be brought into harmony without the subtle threat of inevitable destruction and a kind eye toward an adventurous disregard for safety. That is the way our sales departments and engineering groups need to look at the world. For them, a Steampunk convention is just the right kind of method, or even some artwork to contemplate as the parameters of a new quote show that it will challenge the employees of a current state reality.

It is a delicate line to walk. The time that we best walked it as a culture was when the gunfighters of the American West did so for much the same reasons, technology and ambition fueled human necessity, and a massive jump in culture resulted. The same kind of gates is upon us now. Instead of the frontier being an unexplored plain in North America, it is a space where all the world nations are competing. And to do all that correctly, it will take more than traditional human potential and the concept of conventional morality to pull it off. It will take the kind of raw ambition that we saw once on the Wild West frontier, and as we go to those new places, there is nothing wrong with wanting to stamp individuality upon the machines. In that way, we are genuinely fusing the past with the future and the natural desires of the human race toward untapped economic markets with the ambition to do what people will always do best, to create.

CHAPTER NOTES:

a. Increasingly, technology is a part of any business climate pushing new ideas into traditional production work.
b. As our species migrate into space, the new frontier can only look to the last significant expansion for advice on the thinking it takes to be successful. Untamed profits open the doors for an ambitious tomorrow.
c. People do not want to lose themselves, as happened in the progressive era. This time, people want to see themselves in the expansion as the future comes quickly into our lives.
d. No matter how advanced our mechanical counterparts become, there will always be a need to imagine biological life forms.

THE PINKERTONS

Every major company and many small ones are still reeling over a hundred years later from the Homestead Strike, which involved the famous Pinkerton Detective Agency. The Pinkerton's were hired by Carnegie Steel to break up a union takeover of his Pennsylvania mills. Labor unions were fueled by the recently written works of Karl Marx. They were spreading ideas into the newly created industrial revolution to share ownership of companies between the workers and the owners. Naturally, a significant conflict ensued as the striking union workers tried to storm the mill and drive away the 300 Pinkerton detectives hired to hold them back. Sixteen people were killed and over twenty-three wounded, and eventually, the governor had to call in the Pennsylvania militia to restore order. The Pinkertons themselves were used to this kind of work; they had been doing it since Allen Pinkerton, the founder, worked for the Union Army during the Civil War, supposedly breaking up a Confederate assassination attempt against President Lincoln. As railroads and businesses moved West, the Pinkertons were hired to protect businesses from hostile radicals and became the foundation of our modern-day FBI. Eventually, the Pinkertons would hunt down outlaws like Jesse James and Butch Cassidy and the Sundance Kid, leaving a stain of intimidation on the criminal community that has lasted for the last century. But it was essentially that Homestead Strike breakup that defined them and effectively created a stalemate between business and its workers that has never gone away.

Modern bounty hunters working as consultants use many fancy "Ninja" terms to attempt to tiptoe around the issue created by the Pinkerton massacre at Homestead because the problem was never settled. The definition of this Homestead event essentially shaped modern politics. Most businesses don't want to serve half of an audience; they want to sell their products to everyone. They have never been able to rectify the loss that occurred in the wake of the Pinkerton activity as they continued to instigate violence against protesters. They were themselves outlawed, pushing them further and further West to make a name for themselves, rounding up attackers against the newly established railroads. Reporting directly to the newly created Department of Justice, the Pinkertons were eventually rewarded for their work by becoming officially part of the government itself and the very symbol of law, order, and tyranny.

The fear of the government working through organizations like the Pinkertons romanticized so many confrontations with Wild West outlaws, like Jesse James. Especially in the working classes, people wanted to believe someone could stand up to them and survive. But in truth, the Pinkertons were part of a legal movement that swept across the nation as civilization increased from town to town and brought a sometimes-unwanted order to things that eventually killed the Wild Wild West and left government order in its wake. That was a small prize in the scheme of things as the battle with the unions only ended with a stalemate because of the heavy-handed tactics of Henry Clay Frick organizing the Pinkerton events at Homestead. No matter how justified Frick may have thought they were, the violence gave sympathy to the unionized strikers that carried them through more than fifty years of expansion, eventually consuming most of America's major industries.

The primary problem left in the wake of all this history is who owns a business and decides its conduct, the workers who work in the facilities, or the actual owners—or is the whole arrangement a "partnership?" American business has never clearly defined this problem and has avoided it with bounty hunter jargon that left more question marks for everyone's survival than picking a definitive winner. This indecision has caused much consternation for everyone. It is one of the biggest problems that a modern manager or business owner must contend with within their day-to-day dealings. And it is yet another reason why the proper solution to the matter is to think like a gunfighter.

Before there were Pinkertons, government militia, unionized strikes, and media to shape the stories in favor of public sentiment, there were the gunfighters who used their skills to bring order to chaos, and all these great companies erupted in the wake of that activity. Through honor and innovation, the railroads were created. The gold rush ensued, and that many millionaires were able to carve out a living for themselves across the land of primitive ceremonies and superstition. Without the great gunfighters' humankind would have eaten itself on the frontier without a hint at justice, and society would have ground to a stop before it ever got started. And when dealing with all types of people, even in this modern age, the valor of a gunfighter turned sheriff still holds respect with virtually everyone, even the lawbreakers.

To live an honest life full of merit and when danger presents itself, to face down a bullet intended to end your life, people respect that, and negotiations always go well. The matter has not been settled, but I'll settle it here, owners of companies own their properties, and workers are privileged to work in such places. If they don't like the arrangement, they can go somewhere else searching for ownership more conducive to their sentiments. There doesn't need to be Pinkertons or the government to ensure that one side has an advantage. Management has honest people who will respect everyone and do their best to ensure justice is available even when one or another makes a mistake. Every business in America needs such people in great abundance; it is not up to the bounty hunters or the Pinkertons to protect anything from anything. The company creates value, and it was the business owner who brought the business to life. It is up to the people involved to ensure that the arrangement is not interrupted so that future value isn't lost. But one set of thugs against another, whether it is the Karl Marx union workers or the government-backed Labor Department, what real people respect is honesty and valor. Those elements need to be present in existing management so that when disputes do need to be settled, it isn't some third-party mediator who does the talking. Still, the gunfighter turned sheriff that everyone respects will give them a fair shake.

Valor and nobility were what was lacking at Homestead. Carnegie and his enforcer Frick tried to instill a mass military to do the job of what Frick himself should have been doing as an honest sheriff of the facility. The workers' concept of a business being owned was such an insult to Carnegie that he felt he needed to defend his property from a new kind of frontier robber, unlike Jesse James or Butch Cassidy—the union worker. Union workers born from Karl Marx directly attacked the assets of a company built by industrialists like himself. Doing his fair share of bootlicking, Frick wanted to please his boss with a show of force, which destroyed all civil discourse that might have otherwise been made available to them. In the modern sense, we have many of the same problems, and there is no other solution but to conduct interactions with the workers and the ownership filled with respect. No law in the world or police derived from some deranged economics theorist can ignore the honest sheriff who knows how to fight with a gun but is even sharper with their wits fearless of getting pinned down because they can defend themselves with whatever is needed. Everyone respects a person like that to negotiate with, and to arrive at that level of respect, you must think like a gunfighter.

CHAPTER NOTES:

a. Many companies never got over the tragedy of the Homestead Strike, where the conflict between workers and owners has never been settled.
b. The Pinkertons eventually became the FBI and acted on behalf of a federal view of law and order, as the worker industry was shaped by the newly emerging work of Karl Marx.
c. The killing of the Wild Wild West came forth as the Pinkertons empowered the government to rule over individual achievement.
d. Owners of companies own their properties; it is not a shared enterprise between the worker and management. The company creates value; it is for the workers to maintain it through honesty and courage.

CAPTURING OPPORTUNITY COST

The insults have been numerous; when people say "they are a bunch of cowboys," they mean it as an insult, not a credit. The insinuation is that being a "cowboy" is a reckless endeavor laced with risk and malice. The proper emphasis on indicating that any "cowboy" approach is foolhardy and frowned upon in favor of a more calculated approach to everything is a falsehood meant only to cover the fears of the timid, which are by far the majority in life. By simple democracy, the nervous type dandies of the world have attempted to cover their fears by selling carefully calculated attempts at everything as the way to do things, especially in business, and this isn't the case. There was a reason that great things happened quickly once the cowboys opened markets on the Western frontier, and recklessness had a lot to do with it. Stagnation results from care-driven plans as the opportunity cost is usually lost which is the tragic reality of most business climates.

This concept is revealed all too clearly in the sport of fast draw shooting. As kids, we are all taught to aim and shoot a gun by lining up the sights, taking a deep breath and holding it, letting it out just a bit not to shake our arm, and firing carefully under as much of a controlled condition as possible. However, often time is not on our side, and we are judged in life by how fast we can shoot, not just how accurately, and the sport of fast draw exposes this need magnificently. While practicing fast draw many times, I learned some essential abstract elements to the sport of shooting that often gets missed in discussions. Shooting faster is more accurate than the carefully planned approach, and this is why thinking like a gunfighter can help tremendously in the decision-making process of business in general.

The many ways you can miss under fast draw shooting conditions are getting the gun's barrel out of your holster and pushing it toward the target. Because of all the years of training, the instinct is to bring the gun up to eye level and shoot at the target so sight alignment can be in the realm of possibility. The problem is that under fast conditions, the barrel moves all over the place. The further away from your body that the gun gets, the more opportunity the barrel has to swing around subtly, leaving many feet of trajectory discrepancy at the target to loosen up your groupings.

The most accurate way to shoot fast draw is to fire the gun straight out of your holster, where the barrel just leaves the edge and can be lined up to the target. The barrel swing is at a minimum because of its fixed placement in the holster, and if the trigger is pulled before pushing the gun toward the target, the barrel will be generally stable and not push off from side to side. The faster you shoot in this condition, the more accurate you will be. Now that is easier said than done and can take many hours of practice to learn to trust this form of shooting, but in doing so, speed and accuracy will be significantly improved. It's an odd sensation to overcome because of all our learned practices but is a great example of how pushing through to a new level of thought often requires an approach against our learned behavior.

Often in business, speed is a critical factor in getting an advantage in a competitive field. The seasoned professionals in any industry know how to use their instincts to gain a speed advantage over their rivals. Learning that skill takes practice, just like in fast draw shooting, requires trusting our first instincts over the second-guessing that often drives the decision-making process. Most of the time, it is better to pull the trigger on a decision faster than later. It is not always good to go home and sleep because while analysis is going on, opportunity cost is bleeding away. The good margins are, in opportunity cost, doing things while the rest of the world is sleeping on it. But for that to work, you must trust your first instincts about things, and to develop good instincts, you must have lots of practice to draw from. There is no way to cheat the system; you must do the work and learn from that experience. Once you do, then the benefits of speed are available to you, and don't make any mistake about it; speed and accuracy are the goals.

It is the lazy and insecure person who preaches that "everything takes time." Things do take time, but those who are most successful compress that time into faster segments over others who take too long. While it's true you can hit a bullseye every time you take your time, it is often just hitting the target that we are after in business, whatever that target is. The quality of a bullseye is only an extra bit of icing. So, spending all your time trying to hit a bullseye every time is an excuse for not being fast enough to hit the target to gain opportunity cost, the cost of losing an opportunity to competition by not getting to it fast enough. Speed in business is an opportunity cost. While the timid may sit around the board table and complain about compliance needs that take time, they talk about hitting bullseyes that are not pertinent to the task at hand. When speed and accuracy are needed in partnership, it is better to go faster than slower and aim less physically and shoot by instinct built by experience.

The lazy do not have that experience because they don't like the pressure of shooting fast and still being expected to hit a target. But the experienced shooter knows that it can be done, just as the experienced businessperson knows that the way to capture opportunity cost is to hit the target before anybody else has even thought about shooting. That is the advantage of feeling like a gunfighter in business, shooting and hitting a target while everyone else is just thinking about it. The gain is opportunity cost which often doesn't get adequately measured. What is the price of waiting or thinking and weighing out the options? Usually, the cost is that somebody else will beat you to the punch, which is not suitable for business in any category. While safety is often used to cover cowardness, speed is the utilization of the fortunate. If shooting fast is better, just as in business, the first thought is often the best. Even if you miss if you are going faster than your rivals, you'll get a chance at a second swipe, and you may still beat them. The goal isn't constantly hitting the bullseye; it's gaining opportunity cost just by hitting the target before the competition, which is the key to all endeavors if you peel things away to their basic meanings, especially in the world of business.

CHAPTER NOTES:

a. When people say that someone is acting like a "cowboy," they mean it as an insult and insinuate recklessness about the dominant personality trait.
b. Most business climates do not fully utilize opportunity cost because recklessness is pushed out of a culture. Recklessness is not the problem; it is when the unskilled and lazy attempt to suppress it that much opportunity is lost in culture.
c. Often, the faster you shoot out of a holster, the more accurate you will be because it avoids the barrel swing that often happens when pressure clashes with learned behavior that is not conducive to speed.
d. It is better to pull the trigger on ideas sooner than later because the opportunity cost is bleeding away as the world sleeps.

BE A LEGEND AND NOTHING LESS

One aspect of success that is underexplored but is ever-present in those who achieve it is the tendency to lose your "edge" in the process. It's one thing to enter a gunfight as an untested rogue that has nothing to lose but your life. And if your life is worth gambling to advance yourself, which is often when you have nothing, then the results are not so much a concern. If you lose the gunfight, you die, and that's it. But once you've won a time or two and have things to protect with your reputation, it becomes a whole new story. It is easy for people who have nothing in life to gamble their lives away. But it is not so easy to do so when lots of people start counting on you to win. That is a much different set of circumstances and is a real challenge in another very competitive field. Gunfighting and business reputations mean a lot, and both have extraordinary front-end risks associated with the behavior. It often requires you to gamble much of your life away to achieve the task for anybody who has started a business, and lots of people lose everything in the process. But for those who win, their life is greatly enriched, and something new is born out of that risk. And that is a beautiful thing. However, the beauty can only be enjoyed in hindsight. Fear and terror are often the emotions staring down into the abyss to gamble your life in favor of fortune.

For young people who have everything to prove in their lives and have no reputations for building off of them are often very willing to be reckless because that's the only advantage that they have over their more experienced competitors. But for those who have survived the initial tests of gunfighting or business building, it's not so easy to put it all on the line to do it again. Because once you've won, now you have a target on your back that others want to knock off, and your focus tends to protect that reputation rather than to continue to do the things you did to get to the top. It is much harder to fight with guns that could kill you once you have something you care about losing. But when you have nothing, it isn't gambling away much to go all-in on some significant risk.

Yet, for the great gunfighters and businesspeople of the world, the risk is the natural state of business. Successful people should never seek to protect their reputations and to lay behind them traps for any challenges. The best way to deal with this pressure is to continue pressing yourself to be the best. To take on all challengers more for your benefit than theirs. It is good to continue to feel the pressure of risk even when you are comfortable in life rather than to let the rot of stagnation set in to stop your progress.

Again, poker is the game that best displays this issue. To win the big pots, you must find a way to push up the chip count in the center of the table. You can't go all-in on every round, but you can make a move when you get a hand. You can't just keep placing the minimum bets each round and expect to win the game. You must take a shot when you think you have it and put risk at the center of the game to have a chance to win. You can't just be happy to win a pot or two then sit comfortably on those winnings for the rest of the game. You must build off those risks and continue to push up the pot to win the game. That is how poker is played, and thus, so it is in life.

Once you get your house, cars, family, and reputation, it is not enough to sit in your office and have people gape at your nameplate in awe and spend the rest of your life living off that reputation. You must continue to do things that make people stare and wonder how you had so much courage to continue to risk it all. As you play the game, you learn what risks are worth taking and which ones aren't. But you never stop pushing the edge in favor of risk and rewards.

The experienced gunfighter knows that their opponents are scared and understands how much risk they can handle to be there to challenge. They always know that when the pressure is on mistakes, the more experienced hand will have the advantage in those pressure circumstances. Sometimes people get a lucky shot, but most of the time, not. The skilled gunfighter will meet a challenge in a dusty street, stand in the open fire calmly, and do what they need to win. When Wyatt Earp had to form a federal posse to hunt down the assassins of his brothers, he found himself in a close-range shootout where he was outnumbered. The bullets pierced his clothes in numerous places but never punctured his skin. Earp killed his targets and returned to his life as a cross between a gambler and a lawman. But when the bullets started flying, he stayed calm and let them do what they would. When he shot, he hit his targets, and his reputation lasted while theirs were vanquished. And that is the way of things.

Experience certainly has the advantage, most of the time, so once you win once, it becomes far more accessible in the future. But you can't stop playing the game, and you can't get comfy and just sit on your chips. You must keep pushing up the stakes with a notion to survive your opponents out, and you won't do that hiding behind your reputation. When they challenge you, sometimes you must do like Wyatt Earp and hunt them down and conquer them in a hail of gunfire, and you can't worry about being shot. You must do your thing and let fate take care of the rest. Because often your reputation will do most of the winning for you, once they know who they are dealing with. The most significant value in achieving a reputation is that you can use it for the rest of your life, so the early gamble is worth their life to put on the line for a young person. Because what it gives them will last forever. Yet once you have it, the fight isn't over, not by a longshot.

Whether you are a seasoned gunfighter playing poker in a brothel at the turn of the 20th century telling stories about your past, or a president of some company who had to claw your way over many people, you must understand that there will always be challenges. And those challenges are a benefit. They make everyone in the process better. Yet never kid yourself; they will continue to come for you all of your life. Once you win, they will always come, and you must be perpetually ready for their aggression. The way to beat them away is to keep doing the things you did to get there in the first place and to never sit on your heels and hope for peace. Because peace never comes.

CHAPTER NOTES:

a. Don't lose your edge after you've tasted success. Keep doing what you did to get there, avoiding the trap of resting on your laurels.
b. Once you've won, you will have a target on your back, and that is a new kind of pressure that must be managed.
c. The best way to deal with the pressure is always to take on new challenges; ultimately, you will be the benefactor because the experience will keep you sharp.
d. Managing risk, just like in the game of poker, is how you win in life. It is not enough to win a few times then try to live off that reputation. Continue to risk it all at just the correct times based on experience.

GUNS IN BUSINESS

There are many forums for discussing gun control, and there are many reasons for suggesting such a thing. However, most of them have nothing to do with safety for society but the management of its members. So, of course, this attitude has permeated our business culture, primarily if you work with people from other places worldwide. Guns in America are as they should be, nearly as familiar as a pair of shoes. However, Americans have been made to feel guilty about this trait, and they shouldn't be. Guns and their use equate to freedom necessary for American activities where self-initiation is the key to our culture. Guns protect that self-initiation, so using them even as a concealed carry device is paramount to the overall quality.

America is still a young country, so it is understandable that most places worldwide still have a problem with the foundation of guns across North America. Areas where guns are not standard, have not yet passed through that critical psychological barrier that Americans enjoy, with guns being so prominent even subtly in everything we do. That is why guns should be a big part of our business culture; thinking as a gunfighter helps most aspects, especially in leveraging that always plays a role in any negotiation. It's not in the threat of shooting another person that is the key to this way of thinking. It's how guns make a person feel who knows how to use them and who has them, knowing that tyranny is not part of their life, which is the key to having productive exchanges that everyone can respect.

The animosity toward guns comes from the places in the world that still want to have a top-down management system of their people, from whatever form of government they may have, and having a compliant society that emphasizes obedience instead of self-initiation. There is a big difference, for instance, between a culture that says before a great battle, "let's do it for the king," as opposed to the one that says, "let's kick their ass so we can get some land." One emphasizes sacrifice for the government in power, the other for the potential gains for self that can be acquired due to individual heroics. The kings and queens of the world and the people who want to use their political positions for the same purposes despise the freedoms that guns give people, not in the proposed violence that can come with them. Still, in the protection of self-initiation, such a culture advances.

The same application could be said to be utilized in today's business activities. It is still common for a large company to command smaller companies with a kingly disposition. For instance, if your company falls behind the demand schedule and the big company must come in to push you back on schedule, their approach is usually to make sure you know that they are a big company that could crush your very existence. They say that kind of thing with a smile on their faces. The approach is no different from the many kingdoms of the world who did the same type of leverage upon peasant farmers and street vendors just trying to make a living. The government would position their needs as the paramount concern over the individual requirements for the small business to make a living.

It helps to have a good knowledge of guns and to know how to use them. Even though you probably won't be shooting the antagonists, you know you could, which changes the negotiations' nature. It makes for a much more productive discussion when you know you don't have to listen to any form of intimidation, which helps both parties exchange. Of course, the forces that want to intimidate you into compliance with their demands hate guns for that very reason. Ultimately, what is suitable for everyone should be the focus of any business dealings. The way to get there is to take away the crunch of a larger company trying to intimidate a smaller company. Even if you represent the larger company, it is still your advantage to think this way; you should not be seeking to crush the other person unless provoked. Honesty and understanding should be the goal. The approach of thinking like a gunfighter gets you there faster than in playing the old games of intimidation, of wanting to force others into compliance with threats instead of logic.

One of the most obvious differences between American businesses and everywhere else in the world is self-interest instead of blind obedience. Suppose there is a critical difference in any American businessperson. What makes the Americans the way they are is the expectation that their rights are more important than the considerations of a bigger picture that some out-of-touch government controls. While this is often considered a detriment to most cultures, especially when dealing with businesses in many different time zones, the American approach will get better answers regarding personal responsibility. Everyone in a supply chain needs and respects when doing business a propagator of fearlessness.

In exchanges where a big company must determine why the small company is behind to the schedule if a gunfighter's respect for the other party is used, more honest exchanges can be utilized instead of relying on fear and intimidation to get the results needed. Those types of approaches tend to only favor one side over the other, and in the aftermath, lots of resentment is bred into your supply chain, which is never good. You may get the answers you want in the short term, but you will lose the kind of communication needed to conduct business well and honorably in the long term. People will tell you anything it takes to get you to go away, and once you've gone, they will stop answering emails and phone calls, and you'll lose that honest exchange. But when the meetings from both sides are done like a gunfighter where everyone knows that they can defend themselves from anything presented, honesty has a way of dominating the thought process. Those who want to keep that arrangement of intimidation over others will hate that guns are part of a free society. Still, such a culture is why businesses thrive in the first place because what they make and do is protected by their self-initiation. Once everyone in the business chain is working on the same terms, things work much better than the classic conditions of top-down fear and compliance. Ironically, the point of guns isn't to go out and aggressively kill other people. Guns are ultimately there to let others know that the gun protects self-initiation and that others can't compel the gun owner things they don't think are in their self-interest. While compliance was part of the older way of doing business, this idea of personal self-initiation is specifically an American thing. It comes from the guns in our culture and ultimately is very much a part of how we do business and why. So thinking like a gunfighter is much more productive than being compliant to a more considerable authority and is a key to proper business conduct in any culture, especially those in America.

CHAPTER NOTES:

a. Guns in America are as standard as pairs of shoes, but often we are made to feel guilty about it. So there is a stigma to gun's relationships in business.
b. Guns make a person feel differently about negotiations that everyone can respect because of their orientation toward individualism.
c. The terms in battle stating, "let's win it for the king," are the same types of people who have created the stigma against guns.
d. Guns in business provoke honesty and understanding by removing intimidations from consideration. When self-interest is understood, then rule by force won't be needed.

COMPETITIVE AMBITION IS KEY TO CULTURE

I have been involved in competitive Western arts events for several decades and have met many good people along the way. To me, these events are not much different than other competitive events, whether they may be golf outings or company softball games. However, what is different is that the people who choose to do Western arts types of skills are by their very nature very individualistic in their heart. Western arts presently would not be considered a mainstream activity. Unlike the ambitions of the youth in the era of *The Christmas Story,* young people wanted their very own Red Ryder BB gun because all their heroes on television used guns to instill a sense of justice in the world. There are so many more entertainment options offering even more individual appeal. Those who have typically involved themselves in the Western arts, gun spinning, knife throwing, lasso swinging, and bullwhip cracking, are in and of themselves very individually driven, making competition with these types of people even more apparent as to what truly drives the human soul.

To be an influence leader, the basic foundations of this competitive nature in other people need to be understood clearly because it's relevant in our everyday lives as in our business places. When you become good at something competitively, whether it is something in the Western arts or something as benign as licking envelopes, the nature of other people is that they will use your talent as a benchmark for themselves to chase after. They will, at times, make you the center of their world just so that they can have a chance to beat you. Imitation is something that you should never take offense to; it is indeed the greatest compliment you can ever receive. When people see you as their access to greatness and will work hard to beat you in some competition, you have total control of the situation and provide influence leadership in the most positive way.

What is sometimes hard to deal with is that the people often chasing after you harbor secret resentments, not the kind of thing they will admit in public, but in that they see no comfort in life until they've overcome you. They see no absolute joy until they can say that they've beaten you. In the context of our subject here, Wild Bill Hickock was a lawman who had used his reputation in much the same way, and it forced law and order across the Kansas and Nebraska territories while he lived. Once such a reputation is reached, just winning at the games of life isn't enough, the real challenge is dealing with all the targets people paint on you, hoping to knock you off. When dealing with matters of life and death, Wild Bill was eventually shot in Deadwood while playing poker from behind while holding the famous "dead man's hand," which was two pairs of aces and two pairs of eights, not a bad hand to bet with. He probably would have won that round if he hadn't been shot. But that's how it is with people; if they can't beat you, they plot to get rid of you. Yet when you can make yourself part of their daily thinking, even if it's for malice, then you have gained to a considerable degree control over their lives for the betterment of everyone.

In every place of business, there are competitions. They may not be as apparent as to how fast you can draw a gun and hit a target under the pressure of time or how many targets you can crack with a whip while on the clock, but they are competitive events nonetheless. There may not be trophies involved or cash prizes, but you'd be surprised what people would do for the sheer reputation of winning. Most of the time, a monetary reward is not motivation; the primary driver is reputation. You can see such competitions between neighbors where one gets a new lawnmower that is state of the art. The neighbor will then go out and get an even better one. So it goes between those two, who has the best flowers, the best cars, the best spouses, the best, the best, the best becomes what motivates them toward an elevated state that if the competition were not present, they would never achieve.

Some might point to this activity and state that it is unhealthy to think about such things, but they would be ignoring the basic foundations of how a human being learns and operates. As children, we all follow some examples to learn to speak, walk and set the foundations of our work ethics. The better models, the better we become. But this doesn't go away in adult life. We often put our goals in life based on those around us, and if those people are ambitious, it will push us in a similar direction. In the example of the neighbors with the lawnmowers, the benefit to the whole event is not the lawnmowers or the company that makes them; it is in the lawns themselves. The properties are nicely kept for the people driving by these houses, and people will marvel at the effort, even if the two neighbors secretly want to kill each other over their rivalry. So, it is in business as well, when there are competitive rivalries between companies or within them to deliver superior products, the benefits are in the end consumer. What they get is a better offering than if they had no rivals to contend with. What makes human beings better is competition. And if you are the one who is setting the standards everyone else is chasing, then you are doing something magnificent on many levels.

The most rewarding aspect of getting so good at something other people plot for days and countless hours on end to beat you is that you are the pacesetter for that activity and ultimately the influence leader. Your skill level will establish the quality of the activity, and that reputation will work wonders into motivating people in a positive direction, even in the realm of obscurity. Once you set targets that establish greatness, you will become the target yourself for many others who want to take what you have by gaining reputation. But never fret; this is normal, and when harnessed with greatness is the primary driver of influence leadership. It uses your reputation to drive others toward the goals you want to see happen in thinking like a gunfighter. There is nothing wrong with people who will clamber all over themselves to beat some record that you have established. You generate the ultimate control for setting the goal. If you can get used to the idea that people do not like you for who you are but for their opportunities to beat you at something, then you can gain a great asset to your arsenal of influence. And in that way, you can bring justice to an idea or protect the value of your products by making them better for the marketplace. And it is through competition, these things happen, and people are best controlled toward a positive strategy.

CHAPTER NOTES:

a. To be an influence leader, the basic foundations of a competitive nature need to be understood. People will use your success as the benchmark people chase after.
b. People chasing after you often harbor secret resentments. It is difficult to understand that such malice is at the center of a relationship.
c. If people can't beat you, they will plot to get rid of you. However, this gives you control over the means of their existence. The primary driver is reputation; in the conflict, the world is improved.
d. You use your reputation to set goals you eventually want, and through competition, you push people to achieve your aims and justice to your ideas.

THE SKILL OF DEVELOPED INTUITION

At least currently, when you attend a Fast Draw competition, the first thing you'll notice is that many of the participants are older. Modern gunfighters are older because the cost of getting into the sport is relatively high by the time you buy the guns and holsters that it takes to participate. Other reasons would be that older people remember when Westerns were on television and were frequently part of the movie culture. Young people don't have much to reference when gunfighting, and the cowboys who participated in the activity from an entertainment standpoint are the focus. This might be fine if that activity is just to get together and shoot with some friends. If long-term sustainability of the sport is the objective, then, of course, there needs to be some recruiting going on to bring in young people and get them to carry it on throughout their life. This is the same trait required for all modern businesses; the young should not be looked at as replacements of the old but as assets in sustaining a culture built, whether it's a gunfighting culture or a multimillion-dollar business.

Many people who get up in the years have that permeating feeling that the youth will replace them. Unfortunately, this carries over into all activities that older people participate in. This is particularly true of Cowboy Fast Draw and the various organizations conducting modern gunfights as an homage to their favorite Westerns. While the youth are often distracting with their new bodies, fresh eyes, and aggressive attitudes to win trophies and gain reputations, it can be easier to overlook them and spend time with people who have more shared values as an age group. But honestly, what is needed by the older people is leadership in helping the youth get what they need most in life: reputations. When such a thing is encouraged, a sport like Fast Draw can grow, and a new generation can carry the effort forth. Otherwise, the endeavor will die along with the original participants as the culture will move on from stagnation. This is especially true in sports like Fast Draw, baseball, football, or basketball and business.

The typical business cycle of success that may only go on for a couple of decades is large since companies fail to allow the youth of an organization to grow with wins because the older generation gets used to maintaining a status quo from yesteryear. One of those is, "this is how it's been done and will always be done," the kind of thing that insists the institution's rules are more important than the innovation that is born from competition. Whether it be sports or business, the goal of every competitive event should be to bring forth innovation. For instance, the competitive shooter may have modifications to a holster that may speed up the process or work hard to shorten their reaction times to the indicator light. They may find a better way to deliver a quote or implement it toward customer delivery in business. Innovation is what keeps everything fresh and will carry a business cycle well into the future. However, without innovation, the death of an idea is undoubtedly around the corner.

I am personally a big fan of the work by Mihály Csíkszentmihályi, particularly in his book *Flow.* Daniel Pink has taken some psychological work toward people's true motivations and fine-tuned it more for modern business applications. Anytime a sport like Cowboy Fast Draw is utilized toward a clear target objective, which is the purpose of the endeavor, it creates an evident focus of a mental state to overcome the presented challenges. Performing this task helps the participants be better than a typical state participant would otherwise experience when no competition is present, which is the point of the whole effort. Older people who have already won their trophies and witnessed their name in victory columns will undoubtedly win if they continue to compete. Still, they must understand that winning is not the only objective. Winning is something everyone should always strive to do, but when it comes to the internal development of a culture, that young people are pulled into a kind of Flow state by the prospect of winning. That is their measurable condition for which it can ignite in them a passion;

otherwise, the endeavor will go cold forever. If we try to bring them into the cowboy arts without referencing a favorite television show or movie, they might be encouraged to continue winning a simple trophy. They don't want to hear about how the older guys used to be faster in their youth or that the game is changing so that older people can't compete with younger people through innovation. Besides encouraging competition, the goal of the effort is to inspire young people to find their sense of Flow and carry it to the organization's progress.

In business, young people need to be pulled into the Flow of the business needs in much the way that Csíkszentmihályi and Pink have indicated in their works, but the way to discover it is through pressure's basic reward system. Older people should discover in all their experiences the sheer joy of just being part of the process. At some point through natural growth, they shouldn't care about one more trophy or plaque to place on their office wall; they should be doing their tasks for the sheer joy of doing it and helping young people find that same place of balance within their intellects. In that way, the old should never rob the young of a chance to win. It is up to the old to set up the parameters of victory that the young chase after. It is up to a rewards system to inspire them to continue pushing themselves and refining their competitive necessity. But when all is said and done, the older people can reward themselves with a $100 lunch at their favorite restaurant because they can do that as successful people. Young people still making a name for themselves often can't, so they need a trophy to encourage them to stick with trying to be the best they can be.

The temptation for older people to create barriers to entry, so young people are discouraged from participating, should be avoided in any organization, whether it be a sport or a business practice. Instead, the older people should provide leadership toward the young so that innovation is always taking place. A movement should grow and not decline as more senior people leave the arena. It's not worth a few more trophies to exclude the growth of an idea. In that way, a business cycle can expand and does not just decline once the leaders grow up and away from a task, but it continues and may even improve over time. But only if innovation is embraced over the parameters of victory. While victory is what we all want, sometimes that victory is to survive beyond the expected lifetimes of the participants. That is undoubtedly true of any business. The salesman that lands the big deal once in their life can't expect to live off that fortune the rest of their lives. There should be an up-and-coming competition that pushes for even a better outcome.

The salesperson should be working to put together several better deals during their work life. If someone comes up behind them looking at the targets that have been set ahead of them and do better, that is a great thing for the organization. In this way, the organization becomes individualized and is an entity of its own. And it will only ever be as good as the people who gave it birth. In the Cowboy Fast Draw organizations, that is undoubtedly true. Without the youth, it will not last in the future. But even more apparent is the businesses for which we are all apart. So long as there are healthy competition and innovation, a company has a chance to exist. Once those elements are gone, the prospects for longevity and an end will be in sight anyway. Yet when youth are shown the way toward victory, the ideas that we all worked hard to build may have a chance to last. Success is defined not just in the trophies of the moment but also in the idea's longevity. And that requires that the old embrace their role as leaders and not look at the youth as taking something from them, but giving them what they ultimately desire.

CHAPTER NOTES:

a. For the long-term sustainability of any idea, young people need to be recruited to continue the culture.
b. Older people need to help the youth get what they need most in life, a reputation.
c. Never allow a "this is how it's been done and will always be done" mindset to be permitted to stop innovation. Institutional rules are never more important than fresh ideas of innovation.
d. Young people are pulled into a "Flow" state with the prospect of winning. This is how an organization improves over time and sustains the gains made along the way.

SLAPPING LEATHER OR SWINGING CLUBS

Every time I go to a Fast Draw event, it reminds me of playing golf; the means of achieving victory are not just in the onetime shots performed throughout the day, but the game can take most of a day, and the winner will be the best average of all the attempts. Whereas traditional gunfighters were essentially deadly duels to attempt to restore some honor to a dangerous situation, the sport of fast draw has emerged more as an endurance challenge than a single shot event. The measure of success is not just surviving a difficult moment. Still, in managing speed, accuracy, and endurance throughout an encounter, and in that way, it has emerged as a kind of American sport reminiscent of the Scottish game of golf.

Now I have no beef with golf, it was first played in 15th century Scotland, and it was during this time, the Scottish Rite freedom movement began to influence great thinkers into a new kind of self-governed world, and those two new concepts formed in parallel. Even today, the Masonic movement and golf courses are closely associated with shared birth circumstances. Both came from the same place for much the same reasons. This is also how both ended up becoming part of our modern business culture in the West. Yet, it can't be mistaken that the duels and gunfighting of Western Expansion came shortly after that and emerged from the same kind of need for human freedom, and this is undoubtedly reflected in the games we play as a culture.

However, it's never too late to start. While golf is certainly today a mainstream sport supported by network television and most upper crest communities, gunfighting by culture is not all that far behind. It may seem like a distant hobby played by primarily older people today, but it wouldn't take much to become as common as golf or any other sport. For American business, it may very well be much more aligned. One surprising development that has emerged recently during the early part of the 21st century is a desire to conduct team-building events across the nation with ax throwing and, to a smaller degree, knife throwing. These skills have been around for a long time within Western arts communities but have remained largely isolated from the mainstream. But that trend is changing as people find the need to resurrect the skills of the American frontier so that modern needs of intellect can better be fulfilled.

The gunfighters games have much more in common with the modern businessperson than in golf games, and I would offer that it's only a matter of time before that evolution becomes more widely practiced. In the Fast Draw events, the pacing is very similar to golf, only that the coverage of vast amounts of acreage to play isn't needed. Gunfighting can be done at a central location or even indoors. Yet, the pacing per turn is very similar to the golf game, leaving plenty of time to discuss essential matters between rounds and bonding when playing with friends.

Culturally, and this is something that we are all challenged with, guns still have a stigma placed upon them from global influences and are not inherent in American concepts. Thinking of guns simply as a weapon is to do them an injustice. Each gun comes with its elements of precision that are pretty reminiscent of American ideas of efficiency and tool utilization. So, having a game that unites friends together under a common goal of sportsmanship yet metaphorically helps solve the problems of their livelihoods can be pretty stimulating. It may not work for the European businessperson or the Russian who cannot have guns in their possession or even think of using them for a sport. But for the American businessperson, the objectives are synonymous, and we should not be ashamed of them. Even to the point where our sports reflect that desire rather than look at the gun as some distant weapon of violence from a time long gone with the values we still yearn for.

The games of our culture should reflect the things we do for fun and a living, and in America, gunfighting seems much more appropriate. In contrast, golf was invented during a transitory time for human populations, ultimately evolving the kind of thinking that brought guns about. Once you take away the death and carnage of one-on-one gunfighting but keep the skills needed to compete, what you end up with is a much better mind for American business and the rigors of its daily needs. The tools of the game, the physical attributes needed to play, and the companionship of sharing those experiences ultimately do a lot of good. They should be taken seriously, not as some fringe activity.

The cost of getting into gunfighting, just like golf, can be steep at first, but those costs will come down as they become more mainstream. In the early days of golf, a similar situation existed. There was no Dick's Sporting Goods store nearby, making golf's barriers to entry much less as far as cost. It takes a little time to build a market, but gunfighting could easily be just as comparable, if not more so. The tools needed to play once obtained, the guns, the electronic target systems, the wax bullets, and primers could be performed anywhere, even in a place of business in the corner of the facility that doesn't have a lot going on. It makes for the perfect lunchtime activity. What needs to be changed are the rules against having firearms in the workplace, which is a stigma that must be overcome. Even a golf club could be viewed as a weapon. Single action firearms used in fast draw need to be viewed more as sporting instruments than weapons of war, and once that would happen, the sport could have the opportunity to expand.

The point of the matter is that as American businesspeople, we have attributes specific to our culture, and it's time that we start reflecting on what those are instead of following the examples of the world. We always think of culture for things they are known for, such as tea in England, samurai swords in Japan, and wine in France. Well, in America, it's our guns and how we used them to gain freedom and self-initiation as a government, and those traits are very much a part of doing business with us from anywhere in the world. When we talk about the "American Way," what are we talking about? What is it that we are known for? Guns. So why not make them part of our games and a way to unify our culture from a business perspective? I would offer that we'd all be a lot happier if we just embraced what we are and stood proudly by it in the games of our culture. And we would likely find that other places around the world would enjoy it for their reasons and we could conduct business more honestly as a result.

CHAPTER NOTES:

a. Shooting sports like Cowboy Fast Draw are great in that the endurance challenge involved with pressure present trains the business mind to skills more beneficial to their daily lives.
b. The games of our society reflect the inner needs we share. In that aspect, more individualized sports have increased in popularity, which is part of the story of shooting sports emerging from the games of golf.
c. American business was born from the classic gunfighters, and it's disingenuous not to attach them to what our character is known for.
d. The cost to entry for Fast Draw sports can be steep but is comparable to golf and every bit as rewarding. But the timed element to fast draw gives players more needed emotional depth through the pressure created.

THE CORNER OFFICE

Sometimes there comes a time when a gunfighter needs to be ambiguous. That is, where the fight at hand isn't the fight your fighting, so instead of a noble duel in a dusty street or an emerging city, you must grab your favorite rifle and snipe at your enemies from a distance they cannot react to. Depending on circumstances and, of course, at some point in any growth period where many enemies would otherwise surround you, it is good to take yourself out of the thick of things and take care of business from a vantage point that always gives you the advantage. An example from the morality of the gunfighter would be that you might be facing down a desperate opponent one on one in a duel to the death. If you are the best shooter, or even the most courageous, this one lone gunfighter isn't enough to do you in. However, they may have friends who hide in the windows and every corner and shadow where a noonday sun doesn't shine, and from there, they'll try to do you in while you are focused on the primary opponent. This you cannot allow, ever.

So you've found some success in life and have formed many enemies who want to take you out. Sure they may smile at you and play cards with you in the saloon, maybe even offering to buy you a drink. From all other appearances, they present themselves as your friend. But beware, for such conditions are perilous. Often, not all the time, but too often to ignore, they plot to do you in and will if you give them a chance. It is they who you must watch the most, not always the gunfighter who is in front of you, but the one that is hidden because they lack the courage to face you directly. Those are the most familiar foes you will ever encounter. And if you have been very successful, you will find many such people offering to buy you a drink or polish your shoes.

That is when you must even the odds from a distance and take yourself off the dusty streets, into the shadows yourself. You can take them out when they least expect it and then let the fear of your ghostly menace rule over their reason until they go insane over worrying about where you are and how you will strike next. There is no shame in doing what you must do to live and continue fighting. Surviving is more important than style. Style is great if you can get it, and honor through fair sportsmanship should always be the objective. But you must continue to live to continue playing the game. Getting killed won't do it for you, so do what you must to survive.

Consider that you've been the top gunfighter at your organization for a considerable amount of time. They've even given you a corner office to show their gratitude for all your hard work in taming the business world to their advantage. They will think that by hiring more people like you, they will get even more outstanding results. It's just a matter of time before competitors will be on your doorstep, wanting to fight you for that corner office and to sabotage you at every opportunity so that they can claim jump your efforts to use as their own. These are not just the dandies who come to town later to settle once you've tamed the world for their sensibilities, but these may very well be sheriffs in their own right looking to make a living, much the way Wyatt Earp came to Deadwood and challenged Seth Bullock to become the town's new sheriff. To Bullock's credit, he sent Earp away without much of a fuss, but most great business people won't be so lucky. There will be challenges, and facing them down in a hail of gunfire isn't always the best option, especially if the ownership thinks they did a good thing by hiring them in the first place.

That is where you have to use your corner office or your aforementioned reputation as a trap to seduce them to come near. But when they do, you won't be there, but you'll be off in some corner of the organization watching them and tracking them until they make that fatal mistake. At that time, you either take the shot or let them get stuck in a bear trap they never saw coming as their focus was intently on putting an end to you. It doesn't matter what field of endeavor you are engaged in. These conditions most of the time come from reorganization measures that happen often. Conditions never stay the same for long; what made you great one year may make you a detriment the next to whatever power structure is in play at the time within your organization. Most great gunfighters from the past were criminals in the beginning but ended up as lawmen.

In many cases, once they had been the symbol of the law for a while, they found that they had to turn back to criminal conduct to find justice. Whether it is a town or a business organization, the terms of your employment, most of the time, will constantly be in a flexible condition. To stay in that game, you have to eliminate those who would seek to end you in any way possible, and if you remain in that pleasant corner office, all your enemies will know precisely where to find you and figure out how to dispense with you while they're at it.

Knowing those rules of conduct, every fight you will ever have to win will not be a one-on-one challenge with a noble gunfight pointing to a clear winner. Sometimes you must go even up the odds by residing in the shadows and picking off your enemies one by one or by forcing them to make so many mistakes that they do themselves in. Moving your enemies to destroy themselves is the best option. When you don't have to shoot them with a single shot to reveal your concealment is the best way to even up a score. Yet never be naïve, and don't allow yourself to defend yourself with nobility. When you think you are surrounded, don't be predictable; run for your corner office, and lock the door. Peel away to where they have no idea where you are or what you might be up to. And don't try to shoot them with your pistol; resort to the rifle and use that pressure to force them into mistakes to your benefit.

Under the best of conditions that added competition might be good for the organization, and they may realize in the end that for their health, they must make real friends with you. Not just pretend to get you to lower your guard, and everyone may live happily ever after. But don't be a sucker for hope; make those conditions part of your reality by forcing them under pressure to come to that realization on their own. And in that way, everyone does win. Just make sure it is you who causes it.

CHAPTER NOTES:

a. Sometimes the fight at hand is not the fight we are fighting; sometimes, you must remove yourself from being the target in a prominent location.
b. The more successful you are, the more people will want to appear as your friends, and they will always be plotting to do you in, so they can discover a weakness they can exploit.
c. Surviving is more important than style. Style is great if you can get it, but winning is more important.
d. A corner office makes it easy for rivals to pinpoint your location. Sometimes you must remove yourself from there and take to the shadows yourself so you can snipe away at those you can see trying to enter.

THE POCKET WATCH

Of course, being a gunfighter is not just about shooting guns, but it's in the attitude it takes to become good. Just as in business, if the goal is to be profitable, the gunfighter's concern is to win their fight, and in doing so, you will want to show all future challengers that you must be reckoned with. This helps sort the scum from the gold if you show up for a fight or the events that lead up to a fight looking like a loser who can barely rub two nickels together. If you have shabby clothing and a desperate look on your face, you likely will attract every challenger looking for an easy win. Dressing down does not prevent attempts against you; it attracts them like mosquitos in a swamp. Therefore a successful business person like the gunfighter tends to dress a little better than average to let others know that you are a person who knows their mind and that you tend to go your own way. An obvious giveaway to this type of thinker is to utilize a pocket watch.

Many people don't know it, but the extra little pocket within the pocket of most jeans was put there to accommodate a pocket watch. Even though almost nobody uses pocket watches these days, the standard cut for jeans still incorporates them out of respect for the cowboy tradition of the rugged jeans of yesteryear. The small pocket would hold the pocket watch snuggly until needed so that it wouldn't mix with everything else in your pocket, which might scratch your watch. However, these days there isn't much need for the cumbersome mechanics that make up a pocket watch. Smartphones and many other digital displays of time can now fit just about any place that a pocket can carry them, and they can be tiny and lightweight. That is unless you are thinking like a gunfighter.

Having a pocket watch and using it to tell the time is, in all actuality, a great way to think like a gunfighter. The small gears that are so precise are like the refined mechanics of a finely made six shooter. The windup condition of making the watch work is a constant reminder that in shooting a single-action revolver, it is done so by mechanical means manually driven instead of automation. Plus, a pocket watch is a decidedly profound step away from the modes of thinking that the modern age embraces and lets people know that you are functioning at your own pace.

A human being can shoot a single-action revolver faster than a double-action or semi-automatic in many cases. The cycle time between shots has fewer moving parts in the single action, making it more reliable under combat conditions. That isn't to say that modern-style guns are not better mechanically, but that the single-action revolver still has a place of reliability in the world of combat shooting, just as the pocket watch still tells time as well as any other modern instrument. But with the pocket watch, you can see the mechanics at work and have a relationship with it instead of the digital readout on your smartphone or digital clock that is as flat as a pancake. The result of the action is that modern tools give you one aspect of what you seek, whereas thinking like a gunfighter, you want to have a relationship with the fundamentals of your craft to make the subtleties of things apparent.

Once you start accepting in the world that there are things you don't understand, like how a digital clock tells you the time, you start accepting all kinds of other things that you don't know but yet accept. It is suitable for the fundamentals of your life to be focused on something that you can at least observe or that requires action from you to their activity. Such as winding up a pocket watch instead of just making sure it has enough battery life to continue operating. It is also excellent to know that even if a massive power outage or a battery becomes unusable, a watch will still work so long as you wind it up. That self-initiated task is independent.

Of course, when you pull out a pocket watch during a business meeting to tell the time when everyone else is looking at their phones or in the corners of their computer screens, you are making a declaration of independence that will certainly get attention. And that attention can lead to advantage by separating yourself from the masses so that whatever you say has more weight and respect. The watch itself won't perform any magic tricks, but in your display of it, the concept certainly makes a statement that indicates that you are in command of time. You wind it. You nurture it close to your body but tucked away so that nobody else can see it, and typically all this is done with more amenity than a standard display would accept. So, by controlling time, what else do you manage—your schedules, workforce, supply chain, and margins—everything tends to feed off that pocket watch idea. Usually, the difference between winning and losing anything is the subtle little things we do every day, which our competitors respond to either favorably or negatively. If you want to know the time of day, why not put a little flair to the experience and gain an advantage that is usually lost to our modern world?

Finally, a pocket watch is a sign of affluence, of someone who has been there and done something and came out on top. While this is a cultural phenomenon created by years of movies and games, the impact is real. A pocket watch is like a tie; people tend to respect people who use them, letting other people know that you aren't just some average ruffian who will be an easy victory for their climbs to power. It may make them doubt themselves for just a fraction of a second, but for a person thinking like a gunfighter, that's all the time you need. As a good warrior of modern business, you should take every advantage you can get and earn some of those much-needed style points when you can get them. Style is only essential if it can get you a strategic advantage. Wearing a pocket watch when you want to be able to tell time anyway is a sure way to set yourself away from the crowd while also getting to the foundation of life's very essence. And at the core of relying on yourself to wind your watch, you are, in essence, taking a stand to control time measurement. Not necessarily time itself, but our understanding of it, and that is a mastery all its own. Once you take responsibility for measuring time, you are also responsible for how you can use the time to your advantage in a gunfight or a challenging business deal. And after all, isn't that the point?

CHAPTER NOTES:

a. The gunfighter's concern is winning their fight and deterring all future challengers into thinking twice the next time. In that way, it's good to show off the trophies of success, such as a pocket watch.
b. A pocket watch manually handled takes control of how time is measured instead of the mysterious mechanics of digital readouts.
c. By taking control of how time is measured, it professes that the user is taking charge of other measures, such as schedules, delivery, employee coverage. As a businessperson, this gives a focused relationship to the mechanics of the watch's function.
d. Wearing a pocket watch gives the appearance of being in control of time to those watching your behavior. The difference between winning and losing is in the little things that are lost in our modern world.

FRONT OFFICE POLITICS

Another reason to think like a gunfighter in a business has nothing to do with gunplay or even direct conflict with other people. Essentially, it comes down to a certain kind of awareness that a gunfighter knowing that many people want to kill them, must survive in the modern corporate structure. You must be able to walk down the street with a smile on your face, not scaring all the little children while at the same time being ready to shoot anybody dead who might attack you. It can be a tricky balance, and to get it right in your mind, thinking like a gunfighter helps a lot. After all, especially in American business, where lots of unsaid forces are always in place, conflict is a part of everyday life, especially the higher up in the management structure you become. Just like a gunfighter with a reputation, like Wild Bill Hickok, the longer you live and the more power you gain, the more targets get painted on your back, and you must be ready to deal with them.

We live in an unusual time. Dueling has now been outlawed for many years, and even the notion of carrying a gun is considered radical. Of course, it wasn't always this way, but for the foreseeable future, the honor of a confrontation with someone who disagrees with you has been pushed deep down into our culture to the point where it's nearly invisible to the naked eye. We don't settle disputes any longer with face-to-face contact with an emphasis on a person's honor. Now it's all third-party settlements, lawyers, courts, and the human resource department of our companies. Once the dandies of our world took ownership of production, the means to a living, a new way of killing people has become fashionable—the ruining of their reputations or at least the attempt of it. These days we call it "cancel culture," but that is just a new name for an old practice that replaced the honor of a gunfight to the death to preserve honor and integrity.

For the modern businessperson who must contact hundreds if not thousands of people every day, they must assume that everyone is a potential assassin who would slaughter their reputation in favor of acquiring some measure of power. In that arena of thought, the labor laws of our present favor those assassin personalities and put knives in their hands for the kill. Of course, the whole scheme brings about "fairness" in every workplace, but yet what is empowered is the power climbers who will use those laws to topple their competition. So, a proper mode of conduct is needed to navigate the treachery that is the inevitable result.

The more power you have within your organization, the more challengers you will have who will attempt to use the laws against you toward some outcome of their favor. This might best be considered by the outlaws challenging a sheriff into gunning them down in the streets with little to no witnesses, baiting a court hearing where the sheriff might be relieved of their duty. An outlaw gang may lose a friend to the shootout but what they gain is removing a sheriff in the exchange as the law, then gets tried for murder. It doesn't matter that the outlaws provoked the exchange, only that someone ended up shot, and to instill a measure of the law, the society at large needs a trial and someone to blame.

Certainly the case in all work environments where more laws are established to create victims to flesh out potential targets, the danger is part of the work itself. The intelligent manager and business owner will avoid being pulled into that vortex by not being baited by every little charge that enemies can concoct against you. This skill is as important as being fast and accurate to the draw because knowing when to fight will save a lot of pain later. Enemies don't care if you die a thousand cuts or by just one, so long as you do. Keep that in mind as you interact with teams within your organization that smile at you and address you formally, but they plot and scheme the moment you leave the room. The more power you amass within your organizations, the more scheming and plotting against your name that there will be, so take it in stride and do not be shocked to learn about these occurrences. That moment of shock may put an end to you; there is never time to contemplate such things. Just be prepared to deal with each one as they arise, and be sure to give them nothing to use against you by way of law.

When people talk about fairness, they are not looking to make all hard workers even on the battlefield; they usually indicate that they'd like the lazy to be equal to the ambitious. That is how many of the laws in our human resource realm get written in the first place, so they are not meant to protect you, the high-level manager and owner. So, think of them as if the villains you are there to deal with had written the rules because often they did. Be cautious, especially in dealing with members of the opposite sex, or people from different backgrounds, because laws are written to blow out of context any little phrase or emotional diatribe and frame it clearly in their favor. Think of them all as assassins, and you will be alright.

In Cowboy Fast Draw and other shooting sports, we often refer to the "Cowboy Way" as a method of conduct that will keep you out of the human resource office if followed. Largely the Cowboy Way is not written but implied in most behavior associated with Western thinking, being polite, independent, and ultimately committed. Hopalong Cassidy had an excellent creed for American boys and girls, such as "the highest badge of honor a person can wear is honesty." Or, "only through hard work and study can you succeed, don't be lazy." And one of my favorites, "if you want to be respected, you must respect others. Show good manners in every way." Many others have been written down through the ages, but these three embody most of the variations intended to be a general philosophy for our subject. Treat everyone honestly and work hard, and don't assume that everyone will do the same for you. Independently, give them nothing to use against you and follow that policy logically all hours of the day, even when you think nobody is watching. If you do, your enemies may scheme to get you into human resources to use laws created in modern times to make their killing for them and eliminate you as their competition, but they won't be successful. Ultimately you are in command of what happens to you, so long as you don't turn your back to the dangers surrounding you. Even if you let the pressure coax you into a mistake, it plays into their hands, so deal with the situation knowing the rules and never assume that your friends would never do such a thing. Because if there is the power to gain, even the most congenial friend will become a treacherous villain. Yet, that level of brutality can't be allowed to change you into one of them. It can be tricky business, but if you follow the Cowboy Way, you will always stay ahead of the assassination attempts and keep people looking to you for leadership.

CHAPTER NOTES:

a. Knowing that many want to destroy you in a business climate requires a mindset that embraces the stress of knowing that so many targets are painted on your back, yet you still must walk around with a confident smile on your face.
b. These days, since honor has been removed from our society, a new way of killing people has emerged by destroying reputations.
c. The labor laws of our modern environment have created laws that are the weapons of the day, to take out the powerful by the villainy of the jealous.
d. When people talk about fairness, they intend that the lazy be equal to the ambitious. So think of them as villains who made the rules of the game in a way to assassinate your good name. Follow the cowboy way, and you will be alright.

PUTTING OUT A CANDLE WITH BULLWHIPS

In thinking about the Wild West and its gunfighters, bullwhips ultimately come up due to the nature of mythology that evolved out of stories from the frontier romanticized into modern sentiment and because they were very much a part of Western Expansion. More so in Australia than in North America, bullwhips were used to herd animals from one place or another. It seemed natural when telling modern Westerns like the old Republic serials of Zorro or the Lone Ranger to have the heroes using bullwhips to fend off villains and bring justice to a land of desperados. The bullwhip was my entry point into the Western arts and the first unique skill that I mastered early in life. Over the years, I have given countless demonstrations signifying the effectiveness of the bullwhip to articulate the efficiency and power unleashed by the effect of a handy tool.

When Anthony Hopkins was cracking out candles with his bullwhip in the excellent film, *The Mask of Zorro,* the onset technical crew had to put air tubes on the back of the candles that Zorro was cracking out to show mastery of the bullwhip and the elements of combat. If the Japanese samurai had the precision to cut just about anything with a good samurai sword, the gunfighters of Hollywood's interpretation of the Old West had their bullwhip artists who could put out a candle with the crack of a whip, something that seemed impossible in real life. Yet once I learned to do it, it opened up a whole new world for me because, like many people, I had thought that something like that stunt in *The Mask of Zorro* was just a trick that couldn't be replicated under the theater of reality. In all honesty, when I was a kid, the only thing

I ever wanted to be in life was Zorro or the Lone Ranger. Every other job seemed trivial, and something other people should do.

I learned to put a candle out with a bullwhip after competing in an event for the Wild West Arts Club centered out of Las Vegas, where one of the contests was called the Zorro Board. It consisted of a series of circles oriented in a pyramid shape within a flat board standing upright. What you had to do was precisely target the tip of the candle with the bullwhip through the hole and put out the candle flame with just the sonic boom of the whip crack. In that first year of the competition, I was the only one who did it that day, so I was pretty proud of myself. After that, I put out candles with bullwhips in several venues, mostly in places of business where I was trying to build motivations and teams to accomplish what they thought to be impossible tasks. But I have used the same trick to conduct political points and just pure entertainment. Putting out a candle with a bullwhip for me has always been the most premier example of precision evolving out of American culture. The idea of the Wild West, the mythology of it by the Hollywood industry, and then by actual people who learned how to make the idea into a reality with a fine example of precision by cracking out the flame of a candle by a simple act of raw skill is the defining achievement of western culture.

The bullwhip is an excellent complement to the gunfighter arsenal because it utilizes different skills pertinent to practical thinking and accurate execution of resource management. A gun used in fast draw is a combination of mechanics and science; the bullwhip is about taking science and maximizing its impact. The way of a bullwhip is that the larger tapered end gradually reduces in shape to a very narrow point, 6 feet to 12 feet down the weapon. The purpose of this taper is to put forth a minimal effort at the moment to the handle and to multiply the effort through science to the end where a sonic boom is exposed, where the end of the whip breaks the sound barrier to produce the loud crack that is specific to bullwhips. That sound can then be used to herd cattle where you want them to go. Or, it can be used to demonstrate precision targeting by putting out a candle with that sonic boom.

Understanding how the whip works is needed to understand how targeting something requires a specific mindset of pre-planning that looks effortless in the hands of a competent bullwhip handler.

Subconsciously in the hands of Zorro and the Lone Ranger or even the great Lash LaRue, the heroes using the whip had an advantage over their rivals in that they always seemed to be one step ahead of the villains. However, when the bad guys used a bullwhip, it was always a symbol of power, perversion, and pain. And that is an exciting paradox the weapon brings about in any culture, how its use can be determined based on its character. For the hero, to use a whip to wrap it around a villain is to use precision and planning to stop evildoers. To slice a target out of someone's mouth or to pull a gun from their hands is to show that the mind of the user is so fast that all the calculations it takes to make the arm move the weapon to the coil that makes the crack in a precise space in time are occurring way ahead of the villains. It's almost showing off how efficient the user is in and above the realm of normal. It's one thing to gun down someone faster to the draw; it's another to use a bullwhip to disarm them before the villain has even the idea to pull the trigger.

While the bullwhip is much slower than the typical fast draw with a pistol, to get the whip where you want it under pressure and with so much precision involves many more steps than firing the gun. So to master the art of fast draw, starting with a bullwhip is very helpful. If you can put out a candle with a bullwhip, you can learn to shoot a target with a gun under half a second from 21 feet. The skills are different, but they are similar in putting the mind over tasks that seem impossible. It is still taboo to carry a gun around due to all the restrictions modern society has on them; a bullwhip can be carried just about anywhere. I have taken mine on many flights. I always know no matter where I am, whether it's a fancy hotel on the other side of the world, or performing at competitions in the middle of God's country, knowing that you can put a candle out with a bullwhip rests your mind of other troubles. That is the first step of a warrior's heart. If you can get to that place within your zone of understanding, solving business problems, any business problem, is an easy task. The bullwhip provides a conducive context to any gunfighter in thinking correctly about solving the issues and doing so with great precision.

CHAPTER NOTES:

a. A bullwhip is an excellent companion to the gunfighter and is unique all on its own in American culture. Its display of precision is put to significant effect by cracking out candles.
b. The bullwhip is an excellent example of precision and preplanning by the fast and accurate mind. To hit a target in space and time, a bullwhip is about maximizing the impact of science. To put out a candle with a breaking of the sound barrier right in front of the flame.
c. Precision with a bullwhip showed villains in cowboy-based movies that the hero was always one step ahead. In the hands of villains, a bullwhip symbolizes pain, in the hands of a hero, of preplanning, effectiveness, and justice.
d. You can carry a bullwhip on a plane and, in that way, always have a good weapon no matter where you are.

THE 25/25 RULE

Businesses use many rules of practice to manage their capacities, such as Warren Buffett's 25/5 rule or the International Journal of Production Research's 25/25 rule. With Buffett, he states that out of the top 25 things you want to do in life, you should only focus on the top five until you've completed them. With the 25/25 rule, the goal is to reduce focus on the bottom 25% of your workload. However, thinking like a gunfighter, these measurements in business are only new ways to present targets to hit and have their own sets of useless problems unless looked at correctly. As I have spoken about, there are many weapons that gunfighters can use to do their business; guns are just one of them. Another is the bullwhip which I find has many direct correlations that apply to conceptual business matrixes such as the 25/25 rule.

As I have said about the bullwhip and in fast draw shooting in general, the primary objective is to do the most work with the most power in the shortest and most accurate time possible. With bullwhips, to get the maximum impact out of the end of the weapon with the minimum effort, the handler must project that effort toward a target at an opportune moment where the crack will occur in space and time. It is quite an effort in physics to crack out the flame on a candle with a bullwhip which among those who can call themselves experts is an everyday act. When hitting targets with a bullwhip, the effort looks effortless when done correctly, as most of the action happens within a second of measure. But many small steps within that second must occur correctly to make such a thing happen, especially under the burden of timed pressure. Yet even just cracking out a flame on a candle with all the time to do it in the world takes a very timed approach to inflict the minimal effort to get the maximum results of cracking the whip so near the candle that the sonic boom created blows out the flame.

When companies utilize the 25/25 rule, they essentially say that they are over capacity due to their sales departments overbooking the facility and picking the bottom end of their 25% of the business portfolio to ignore. That way, they can focus on their top percent of valuable customers. This approach allows lousy management to hide behind a measurement method and use the analysis to disguise inadequate approaches to solving the problem. In the Cowboy Fast Draw competitions and Wild West Arts work, the weapon handler needs more time to do a good job. But as we know, in gunfights, the fastest and most accurate were the ones who won the duels. There were no rules for taking time to deal with the incompetence of the duelists. If the gunfighters were incompetent, they were killed. And the same holds in business.

The aim of the Western Arts isn't just to enjoy the historical nature of traditional weapons used in war within American culture. Still, it is to represent the necessities of living within Western society. American business needs are one of those requirements, and not connecting those proper metaphors to the function of the business can lead to a detriment, which for too many companies is a common occurrence. Such as the case with the 25/25 rule is the way it has been proposed to help companies with overcapacity problems. The solution to those problems is experienced in a Western competition where speed and accuracy are measured. There are many outstanding shooters in the world and excellent bullwhip artists who have trouble with the fast draw competitions of Western Arts. They look great when performing for audiences until the pressure of time is added, then things get tough, and people start reacting poorly under duress, which is the point.

Most United States and European consultants follow similar methods of reducing "push" systems and instead incorporating "pull." One element of a supply chain does not ship until the downstream source is needed. The 25/25 rule is an element of this thinking, and it essentially dances around the actual villain, which is incompetence. If a manager, either upstream or downstream, just can't handle the pressure and has a hard time recruiting and retaining good employees, they will have trouble doing the required job. The 25/25 rule gives them some cover to focus only on their valuable customers and let the less valuable fall off the portfolio. This might look great for the internal measures of a production environment, but it doesn't equal the task of the sales department that is trying to book work and help a company profile with new business. The incompetent managers within an organization might be angry toward sales for bringing in more work than they feel comfortable handling. And that is the core of the problem. Many of the Lean consultants do have good ideas. Still, they try to use peer pressure to level load a facility's production output instead of focusing on making the individual contributors better.

I have seen many outstanding bullwhip artists struggle with the speed and accuracy competitions in Western Arts events. The rhythm and pressure of a timed competition throw off everything, and they would argue that if the rules were not so rigorous, they could do better if only they had more time. Well, who couldn't? The point of timed pressure is to sort out the good from the bad, and business is indeed the case. Thinking like a gunfighter, anything less than fast and accurate would mean death, and it does to businesses also.

It is up to the weapon handler, such as in the bullwhip artist, to get better, to acclimate the practitioner to the conditions of the battlefield with improved skill. If doing a speed and accuracy competition with bullwhips between 15 to 12 seconds is the parameter needed to win, then that is up to the bullwhip artists to compete in those parameters. In businesses where sales provide jobs, and the various program managers within the organization determine that the scope of work fits within the company portfolio, it is not up to production's weaknesses to decide that they can't live up to the expectations. They must get better to meet the needs, not hide behind some bounty hunter rules created to make their business thrive while the firms that hire them suffer under their incompetence. Rather than force the industry to deal with the artificial constraints created by bad management, companies should strive to get 25% better to meet those market needs and create value for their customers. What if a town sheriff stated to the population looking to them for protection that to be a good representative of the law, the criminals needed to be 25% slower in their threats? Actions of aggression also need to be reduced by 25% so that the sheriff could handle the dangers? Instead, it is up to the sheriff to get faster and to be better. And if more bandits come to town and are more intelligent and faster yet, it is up to the law to get better to keep the peace. So, it is with any business. The customer needs what they need; it is up to the company to give it to them without going out of business. And that only happens when you force everyone to get better, not playing to the weaknesses of the workforce managed poorly by the incompetent.

CHAPTER NOTES:

a. The 25/25 rule states that you should not think about the bottom 25% of your business portfolio to avoid overcapacity problems.
b. Not accommodating capacity challenges is a display of not having the willingness to gain the skills to deal with 100% of capacity challenges.
c. These kinds of capacity justifications allow lousy management to hide behind methods of measurement that look sophisticated but are intended to conceal incompetence.
d. The solution to capacity problems is to improve skills to accommodate the marketplace. It is not yielding to incompetence.

GAMBLERS RUN THE UNIVERSE

I've always had an uneasy relationship with casinos. On the surface, they are what they are, dins of evil that bring out the worst of human behavior. Under the lawless conditions of the Wild West, it was no surprise that they sprung up in just about every civilized town where people had money in their pockets to spend on behalf of the house. Yet, there is specifically in American culture a love of casinos that goes to a more profound meaning directly connected to our business climate. Part of the romance of the Wild West period was that ordinary people could risk it all without the confines of social tiers and become wealthy and independent, panning for gold or gambling in the frontier towns of Western expansion. Most fell short of their goals, but everywhere that cards were played and gold was panned for, there were opportunities for personal enrichment. In that fashion, casinos are an accurate window into the true motivations of human civilization.

Thinking like a gunfighter, risk and rewards go hand in hand. It's not by accident that many of the best gunfighters who grew in fame were usually considered great card players. And it's also not a coincidence that some of the best gunfighters also tried their hand at legitimate businesses. Like card playing, risk and rewards are the name of the game in business. While many modern bounty hunters preach to their flock that good business is risk aversion, it must be understood that the only benefactors of that advice are the bounty hunters and the dandies who hire them. It's not for the good of the business. Business, all business, comes about from risk and the rewards that come with it.

Over time I have come to see honesty in casinos that are part of the rooted foundation of American life and business, the raw ambition to step out above one's station to gain independence. Let's forget for a moment that all casinos exist to make money for their owners. But they do have to let some people win to keep people coming back for more. And for that little chance at hope, people are willing to risk it all to advance themselves. In that is something very specifically American and at the heart of American capitalism.

Religious leaders and government types like to earn extra tax money off gambling efforts, but just enough to keep people more focused on the lights and buffets, and not the winnings, demonize casinos and their gunfighting founders as beyond moral conduct. Until it is realized that morality is defined by compliance and not financial reward and the freedoms that can be born in their wake drive all human behavior, then no civil culture can percolate. Of course, where the easy money is fashioned, looters with evil intent often follow, like prostitution and other pursuits of sheer pleasure, but what is missed is the essence of the urgency to gamble, to take risks to get rewards and the addictive thrill that comes with winning.

All gunfights are a gamble; even a great shot could miss just a bit, luck might be with the challengers that day, and a deck of skills stacked in the gunfighter's favor may not be enough. So even under the best of circumstances, it's always a gamble to bet your life against another. That sense of raw emotion still lives in many casinos where the high rollers aren't necessarily wearing guns at their belt. Still, they have the same swagger and self-confidence forged under pressure and a reputation of victory that follows them often for years. Many people will kill to have that reputation and to get it; many people must risk death literally and figuratively to get their hands around it and have a chance.

As is the challenge in every casino, the challenge in every business is that banks don't like risk, especially in large established organizations. Much of the focus of all company efforts is on risk aversion, not on risk implementation. The house is stacked against the hopeful gambler, and despite those efforts, we need in every capitalist enterprise risk-takers who will try and put themselves on the line to produce something from nothing in the hopes of getting rich. If that hope is not present, what is there for them to create work to begin within a business? All businesses need dangerous risk-takers to advance their cause. As every gambler knows, you cannot just sit on your chips and play everything safe and hope to succeed. At some point, the chips must be gambled in hopes that they'll strike gold and have a chance at independence financially.

Casinos have all the bright lights and images of gold because in each of us, especially in the United States, risk-taker mentality and such things appeal to our senses. Some people can manage that thrill, others struggle, and the best find some happy place between complete insanity and calculated prudence. Never tell a banker of those traits; they will lose countless hours of sleep and deliver you a sharp interest rate. But when it comes time, just like our ancestors' gunfighters, sometimes you must face down death itself and expect to come out on top of gambling your life in the process. In some cases, the threat to life and limb is literal; in others, it's a possible bankruptcy, but at some point, all businesses to be successful require somebody to take a significant risk. To bet it all on success, on plucking from a stream a gold nugget, or winning that big poker hand in a smoky saloon. But to even get at such tables, it will cost you money and possible reputation.

American business is different from business in other places because the memory of Western Expansion and the possibility of financial freedom still hold people the dream of waking up without worry each day about how to pay their bills. It is alive in America because other places still have overlords and monarchs who essentially still are a factor. Even people who achieve financial freedom still must bend the knee to someone. But in America and for the American businessperson, there was a chance that if they did achieve financial freedom, they could have individual liberty. The opportunity for that chance fuels many of the great things that we enjoy today from all the many businesses of American culture, everything from the latest toymaker who invented the small little rubber thing that puts a smile on the face of a child to the most recent iPhone.

To think like a gunfighter, it is imperative to have a gambler's relationship to risk and to not run from it, but to run to it. To embrace it like you might a spouse under the more tender aspects of a relationship, risk and love are the same. From both come something new, from the spouse, children, and the business, opportunity. And sprinkled everywhere in every casino, some players are brilliant, some dumb as a rock.

Still, with equal opportunity, the chance for a big break at independence is very much at the core of the human experience. And it can be seen best in casinos and disreputable establishments of bright lights and degradation shadowed by lawlessness. Because it is in such places where the honest heart of all human beings can be seen without the tapestry of rules and regulations, which can make the deceitful appear virtuous. When it's all on the line, the pressure is honest. Under such pressures, the best of who we are rises to the surface. Risk and functioning under the pressure of it are what make businesses great. Then comes the challenge of holding what you've won, which is another problem. But even there, the risk is part of the game. You can never rest on your laurels.

CHAPTER NOTES:

a. Casinos, on the surface, are dins of evil that have sprung up out of a deep need humans have for embracing risk in their lives.
b. The idea of any individual gaining wealth stepping over the social tiers of control is an exhilarating prospect, even though most people will lose fortunes in the process.
c. There is honesty in casinos that represent the needs of Americans and their businesses in a way not otherwise measured.
d. If the hope of wealth through risk is not present, then there is nothing to drive business leaders to create industry. In casinos, risk-takers are unleashed, and we can see their spirit and the health of our culture.

SEEING WHAT IS INVISIBLE TO EVERYONE ELSE

One of the most sought-after traits in business and life, in general, is vision—the ability to see long and far into the obscurities of existence. Many studies by many, many bounty hunters claiming to have the secret sauce for vision, attempted to catch it in a bottle. Whether the endeavor was called "Lean" manufacturing or the "theory of constraints," vision to see the obscure is always the promise, but seldom are any tangible deliverables ever obtained. For example, many consider it one of the Wild West's most significant acts of villainy when vision overtakes the meek and scrappy. Many modern political pundits do as well and for the same reasons. George Hearst was a very powerful businessman as opposed to the desperate gold diggers hoping to fall into good fortune with some level of vision that one had which the others didn't. Lots of bounty hunters working today, among the many businesses of our concern, are also selling some form of snake-bite remedy they claim will help their contractors see better. Which, of course, never works.

Imagination is one element of vision, and for the imagination to work best, a mind must be accessible. A mind not conquered by the necessities of existence can think of abstract elements unencumbered by needs for survival. Since most everyone does not have such luxuries, vision is complex for them; it's hard to see beyond their immediate survival needs, so their imaginations never develop beyond basic urgencies. The other element that is needed for proper vision is a sense of fearlessness. Being afraid of things puts the mind into a primal condition of survival, therefore impeding the abilities of vision. For most people of great vision, these two elements are found hand in hand. That was certainly the case of George Hearst and many along the Western frontier. They used the freedoms found in an unsettled land. They combined them with the brutality of being at the top of the food chain intellectually to unleash great business development attributes.

Those who do not have vision or are plundered with a constant sense of fear may look at people like George Hearst as a villain, a minor stakeholder, and a politician who gained a lot of power over his lifetime. Since losers often define villains and winners the heroes, a tie-breaker is often needed. Their accomplishments measure those who achieve while the debate will rage on other values such as sentiment, compassion, humbleness, and altruism are tossed in to describe a complete human being. Those attributes often have no bearing on success, whereas success has value to everyone that it touches. Vision is the ability to see value where nobody else yet can. That ability may be considered ruthless to the blind but a boon to the enlightened. Yet make no mistake about it, the ability to see with "vision" is more valuable than gold or any other great wealth because it is the crucial ingredient to wealth creation and business fortune.

Vision is not something you read in a book and acquire; it's something you develop when your mind is free, and your body isn't afraid of being shot in the back because you are either faster to the draw or better equipped in life to insulate yourself from attack. Hearst was powerful by becoming a politician in San Francisco during the 1860s. He had developed his famous Homestake Mine in the 1870s in the Black Hills of South Dakota, which produced gold until 2001; he was thought of as a great visionary. The gold had always been there, but it took a mind like Hearst to extract it from the ground and make something of value from it. To those who weren't so visionary, of course, Hearst was a villain, just as many business people often are viewed by those who can't see so well. Hearst developed his vision not so much at gunpoint personally but in using other mechanisms of power, particularly political interests, to remove barriers to market entry and create something from nothing for which produced value.

Walt Disney was another great mind of vision. He didn't need to carry a gun to protect his imagination. Still, he did have several well-known run-ins with the type of greed that can ruin people for life, as he developed his idea for Micky Mouse and became fiercely protective of his creation over the years. For that is the reality of people with great vision, whatever the weapons of their day are, whether trademarking, fistfights in the street over a gold claim, or a literal six-shooter at your hip, visionary people need protection so that their imaginations can wonder over the possibilities. They need to do what nobody else can, even with the same ingredients right before their faces. Many schools and mentor programs could be easily duplicated if they could be easily copied and would love to recreate a Walt Disney or a George Hearst at will, but they can't. The bounty hunters hope that they are paid and gone before consumers find that the snake oil sold to them for vision was simply a complex liquor with no magical properties whatsoever, only drunkenness. And like the fools, they are hungry for a way to pay for success; the bounty hunters are hired repeatedly and tricked that many times over due to their failure to understand that vision is a developed trait, not an acquired purchase.

Vision also is a lonely attribute. It's not like relationships with other people will increase a person's vision. If anything, it limits it and pulls the seeker back into that primal void where necessities are clasped like a drowning person avoids death in a frozen river. Companionship does not make better vision; it distracts from it. With that said, the lonely gunfighter cleaning their guns around a campfire just outside of town is more likely to experience great vision as opposed to the drunk gambler hanging out in a saloon and clamoring for prostitutes upstairs with the winnings. The peace seeker striving for companionship will most of the time lose to the gunfighter indifferent to relationships. Vision-like leadership is not a shared experience. More people do not make the likelihood more probable of their occurrences. Vision is a solitary gift by those ruthless enough to step over the need for primal necessity or those so bound to their imaginations that their guns keep them from the harm of prying villains' intent to steal their time and effort.

There is no shortcut to sight; learning to see only comes from imagination and the solitude of self-mastery. Great visionaries through history were not those clamoring at the social clubs looking for advice; they were alone with their thoughts and well-developed imaginations to forge new ideas on the frontiers of innovation. And to get there, they had to find a way to place a barrier between them and the parasitic natures of the blind, with either great power obtained socially, politically, or some other means, or a trusted gun at their side. The ability to ward off theft physically and mentally is the key to developing vision. It's no miracle tonic that you can purchase from a bounty hunter; it comes from experience, imagination, and fearlessness. And to be free of fear, a means of self-preservation is necessary. For the gunfighter, it's in knowing how to shoot their gun. And at whom when needed, metaphorically or otherwise.

CHAPTER NOTES:

a. Vision is one of the most unique attributes of a successful business. It is born from leadership and independent minds who think on their own.
b. A mind not conquered by the necessity of existence provides the free will to produce vision in the imagination.
c. Losers often define villains and winners the heroes, success is valuable to everyone, but everyone does not create it.
d. To those who weren't so visionary, George Hearst was a villain. But it was Hearst who came up with better ways to extract gold from the Black Hills of South Dakota, which is why he was very wealthy and successful.

MYSTERIES OF ENGAGEMENT

One of the most mysterious problems in all business activities is the engagement of the participants in the task at hand. Measuring engagement is a nightmare for even the most outstanding organizations because there is a fine line between compliance, doing what one is told, then generating interest in an ultimate resolution for the sake and beauty of doing it. Following up on an email or the action items after a meeting requires engagement in the process to advance a topic. Often, getting employees to invest themselves into the outcome is difficult at best. Most unskilled managers will resort to threats transferred through the rank to achieve their desired result, such as would be seen under any Theory X management style. Then, of course, Theory Y is all too free-flowing, to the point where the mind may be free to function, but the code of conduct is reprehensible and undisciplined. The fight to maintain that balance is an ever-present challenge that the scope of a vision will completely control.

It is not by accident that so many inventions and businesses erupted into being during Western Expansion, led by the gunfighters, gamblers, and gold diggers that fled the authority of civilized society for the possible adventures offered during that period of time. It was upon those endless vistas that extended into the vast horizon that those with significant vision could conceive of railroads spanning the country and inventions of all kinds that would launch the Industrial Revolution. It was no coincidence that the friendship between Seth Bullock and Teddy Roosevelt would lead the president to great acts at the introduction of the 20th century. They were taking a great vision and applying it to push forward the Panama Canal, the Rough Riders in Cuba, and the start of the most significant military power on earth. The American West's big sky ignited big thoughts that permeate today. Obviously, in places like Las Vegas, and can be seen clearly while landing in Dallas, Texas, over the many bright blue swimming pools and oil fields, the residents' apparent signs of great wealth were exhibited.

Unlike other places in the world where no gunfighters came to tame the land from heathen sentiments, such as in Siberia, Mongolia, or the Middle East, such an experience of justice during the gold-rushers had never occurred. Except for what Mohammed bin Rashid Al Maktoum has been able to do in Dubai, nowhere in the world was such significant economic expansion seen where long horizons freed people's minds to think in big ways about big things to the point of incredible creation. As has been the trend for millenniums, human beings have compelled themselves to city-states where the limits of their vision were their creations of buildings and religions. Once established, the natural inclination was to form the patterns thus established. The buildings might have erected taller, as they did in New York over this Western expansion period. But the daily thoughts about things came from the West and the need to reach for more gold faster and more efficiently.

Where profit wasn't the motive and opportunity thought to fantasize about, the horizon has largely remained unchanged throughout human endeavor. Whether we are looking at the African plains or mountains of Siberia, many of the same features found in the American West can be seen, yet nowhere near as developed. Anti-capitalist forces of modern politics may see this as a benefit. Still, as a business is one of the most creative of all things a human being can do, more so than painting a picture or sculpting a new statue, any hindrance to business practices is a knock against the purest form of art in the world. The making of a product and the fulfillment of a customer to buy it. Even visiting the great Louvre in Paris will reveal that all the art efforts over the many centuries have never yet nor will they ever equate to the creative potential of the businessperson. And nowhere on earth was the potential unleashed as it was behind the guns of the American Gunfighter.

To have a vision, as has been mentioned, a person must be free of fear, but to have a large scope vision, a person needs to look at the world and see beyond its restrictions. Still today, the American West does that for anybody with the eyes to see such a thing. Looking at a horizon and seeing a blank page of opportunity that could unlock any number of possibilities in the human imagination is what makes humans unique, even among members of our species. Such thinking helped along with the start of American business and the magic of the Industrial Revolution. It unleashed the lack of limits that explorers, gunfighters, and early settlers moving west of the Ohio River found. It established Chicago, Detroit, Cincinnati, and St Louis into launch points for business and enterprise. Revisionist historians with hindsight analytics will emphasize the mistakes made in this period, the long hours, the child labor laws that were not yet in place, and even how the land was designated as owned. But those efforts can't erase what was made from the blank sheet of paper presented and the great art of business produced, which we take for granted to this very day. Ancient people settled the American West for those same millenniums and did nothing with the land but push around the dirt in dedication to ancient religions. Once the gunfighters had cleared the way of the West of fear and anxiety, the scope of imagination had room to grow, and so it did, in spectacular ways.

In this way, thinking like a gunfighter allows the businessperson to think beyond limits to increase the scope of their vision by looking through artificial barriers. In many ways, modern business is a maze of barriers to entry, many designed to keep establishments in power and newcomers spending themselves into oblivion to get a seat at the table, which dispels them from productivity once there. That is where a certain amount of healthy ruthlessness must come into play. You may not gun down your opposition to entry so that you can see through to the scope of your vision, but you will have to think of your enemies as things to overcome, not to make friends with. To achieve a grand vision with a large scale scope, sometimes it happens so fast that the market can't react in time to stop you, such as what happened with Microsoft and the many startups in Silicon Valley. But usually, the markets you are trying to work with and innovate into a new future state have gatekeepers who have created lots of barriers for you to jump over or crawl under. That is when you must think like a gunfighter and clear out the villains, and once past those barriers, the infinite possibilities of the human imagination can take root and make things that nobody thought were even possible. Just like in the American West period of expansion, it's not the land claims and human labor perils that we should be thinking about; it's the great things that came from that period to give us all a new reality. In the end, that is what all businesses endeavor to do, which is one of the most beautiful sites in the world. And once free of barriers, people will be more engaged once they see that the smoke has dissipated and the villains there to steal their thoughts are gone.

CHAPTER NOTES:

a. Measuring engagement from their employees is one of the most challenging things to measure in any organization. The trick of engagement is to figure out how to get employees to commit themselves to a task beyond the standard measure of pay.
b. Previously the limits of vision and engagement were in dedication to the needs of a city-state. Profit wasn't the motive, but loyalty to the rulership was. That is why they eventually all fail.
c. A businessperson has the best expressions of art of all the great works in human history. It was the gunfighters who cleared away the state commitments and unleashed individual enrichment.
d. You must think of your enemies to be overcome, not to yield to. That is how vision is born from engagement; when the villains are cleared away, the human imagination can express itself for the great things which emerge from the invention.

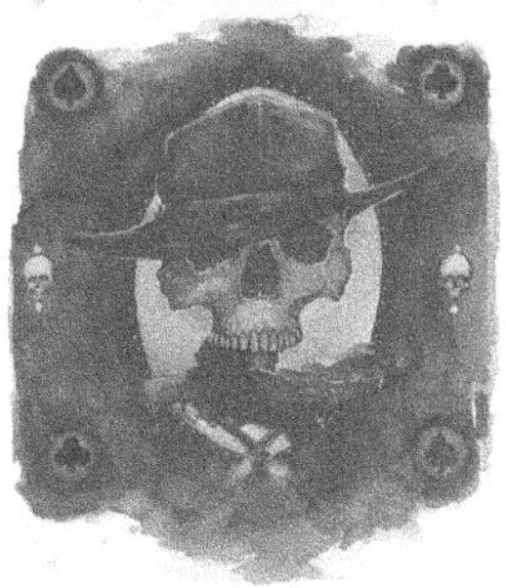

THE VALUE OF A STORY

Something that has emerged in modern construction projects, particularly in architecture, is the notion of creating a fictional narrative behind a project to unify all the participants into the overall scope of the endeavor. The Disney Company comes to mind in their work, particularly in the Orlando area, with their most recent undertakings. For instance, for their highly successful Disney Springs shopping and entertainment complex, they have created a fictional backstory to keep all participants focused on the project's scope and unify the vision for an overall effect. I can think of a similar shopping complex near my home that has attempted to do the same without the benefit of the fabulous Imagineers who work for Disney—yet the effect has been similar. Human beings interact with the world through a story mechanism that is the foundation behind all economic activity, religion, and even the social sciences. It only makes sense that stories and a narrative should be mastered to the optimal effect in business.

Context is another aspect of Western Expansion where a narrative drove the effort. When people from the east coast learned through newspaper stories and dime novels of the adventures occurring in the Western territories, it drove imagination and, therefore, investment into joining that adventure sometimes at all cost. This accounted for the droves of settlers who braved a new world and all the dangers associated with opportunity for something unique. Whether it is the modern Disney Springs promising something above the average for the consumers partaking in activities there or the dusty streets of an old Wild West town, a storied narrative is always the driver of investment and innovation.

When it comes to the gunfighters of this period and our modern memory of them, many stories spawned off their efforts, true or not. The result was a desire to participate in that story, even if it only meant opening some lonely shop on the frontier where those stories occurred. The importance was not whether the rumors were true but in the impact, it had on the imaginations of those hearing about those antics. As many who think of these kinds of things understand, reality is determined by how the brain interprets information, whether it's a dream of randomized events brought to mind through reading, observation, or even taste instead of recorded statements of fact they occur. What the mind sees through senses often determines the reality of the participants, so a good story can unify the minds of many toward the abstractions of interpretation by providing the same information to the masses.

By nature, gunfighters were the center of attention in the period of Western Expansion. Defying death or dying in a blaze of gunfighting was always the subject of a good story, and for good or bad reasons, a narrative would form that would then be conducive to economic activity. Of course, we've mastered this trend in our modern world, where stories are given to us with virtually every television commercial, movie, or internet ad. There is always some tie-in to a greater narrative that becomes synonymous with the brand of a product. But the first time in all human history that this happened in near-live time was during the Western Expansion days where railroads could carry mail from the country's interior to markets in the east within a few days instead of weeks or months. Suppose there was a deadly duel in Deadwood streets. In that case, citizens of New York were reading about it within the week, and lonely ladies and men of adventure were eager to join the drama with plans of their own. Thus, economic investment exploded, and so did the efforts of innovative enterprises.

Good and bad new endeavors sprung up across the frontier as the fertile mind of human beings from all casts of life sought to make a name for themselves. The fantastic Western adventures reported by the newspapers and novels are natural for all people to gain context for a vision. If the natives of previous generations were content to live with the stories of their mythology of religion, of the animal relationships to the cosmos, the modern Western expansion of the gunfighter taming nature and making their creations were dominating the landscape and changing the nature of economics forever. It wasn't the greed of humankind that propelled such an enterprise, but the point of a gun and the ability for the first time to make one's way with bravery as the only wind in their sails. Thus, many stories were born and reported of these efforts that excited those seeking the same. This yearning remains to this very day in just about every product on the marketplace. It was easier to focus on the gunfighter age because the information flow was going in one direction from a specific group of adventurers. Today the information flow is a bewildering maze of material in all directions about every topic, all hours of the day, all days of the week, every month of a year. It never stops, but the results and birth of the ideas have never changed.

Thinking like a gunfighter, it is essential to understand that the pinnacle element of leadership that nobody teaches these days is that by creating a story and allowing people to rally to it, you give them something to believe in. Suppose it's just your reputation for gunning down villains or the propensity to want to do so in the future. In that case, that is part of a story that followers can rally behind, and they will work with great enthusiasm if given the opportunity. For those who conduct their lives with a narrative that others can follow, natural leadership can be said to be working its full effects. It's not so much crucial whether that narrative is true. If it is, that's better, but what counts is that people can follow a story that a leader creates. And in thinking like a gunfighter, that was half the battle of building one's reputation and becoming synonymous with history, which many of them were well aware was their fruitful task in the end.

There is always a story to be told in the modern business environment. Whether our task is a form of VSM or a presentation on PowerPoint to a board of directors, you must always find the story of the situation and tell it in a way that inspires action. Gunfighting was always a grand entry to telling stories of American frontier life, but there can be a story in anything. Mythology is more critical to the human mind than the truth; what matters is that you capture other people's imaginations in a way that inspires the creation of something new and tangible. Thinking like a gunfighter, it's not so much about shooting down villains who stand in the way of progress, but the stories that catapult them into fame later as the stories are interpreted with a flair that was typical of second and third tellings, and soon after that they became legends. And when it comes to leadership, legends are always easy to follow and get the funding for their antics.

CHAPTER NOTES:

a. Most things that humans do are to create a context for their endeavors through the value of a story.
b. When an enterprise can put tasks to others in the scope of a story, then the value can be seen by those who don't naturally possess such vision.
c. Investments for any endeavor are often solicited best through the context of how profit will spawn off a story.
d. Reality is often determined by how a mind interprets information, not necessarily by the facts of a matter.

ONLY THE TOP PEOPLE

There are standard terms used in modern business all the time, statements like "stay in your lane" and "respect the chain of command." That is one of the dumbest things any gunfighter could do when coming to a new town and looking for villains to eliminate to bring peace and justice to the nature of things. You would not go into a saloon while inquiring about villainy and ask where the bad guys are because most of the people there would likely put up their hands. Instead, you must learn to find the top people and to associate with them in whatever you do, at the highest rank. You don't waste your time with the losers spitting in the spittoons and wasting away in the bosom of a whore; you deal as high up the food chain as you can so that the strings of power point to the controller you need to be dealing with. If you associate with lowlifes, the path to justice will be long and elusive—and the system is set up to hide those truly at fault, so likely, if you follow the house rules, the villains will always prosper.

Of course, concerning business, the rules are the same as they are in any culture. If the goal is to improve a situation, and to be the most profitable, if you want to get to the movers and shakers, you don't waste time on those asleep in the corner or performing gossip about what they think so and so might be doing behind a locked door. You make sure to get yourself behind the locked door so that you can find out for yourself. If you stay in your lane, as they like to say, you will discover that they'll block the road from your ambitions, and your hunt for justice will constantly be thwarted. Justice is in the realm of business, a profitable enterprise that is efficient, speedy, and delivers what the customer wants. For a hired gunfighter, the customer wants villainy eradicated so that people can live in peace and enjoy their lives without worry. The same is true of any business, people want to be employed, and employers want the people under their care to be happy and stay with them for the long haul.

Contrary to what many are taught, mainly by the villains in the saloons and advocated by the bounty hunters always looking for work, businesses want a happy workforce. They don't want to continuously replace people or struggle through cycles of growth and decline; companies as much as possible want steady growth and to keep their gains. That means, preferably, by their instinct, businesses want a good culture that lasts; not only is it good for business, but it's good for any company's future growth. In the Old West period, robber barons were given a horrible name by political papers looking to victimize subscribers into hatred for the easy targets of their employers. Every little move was heavily criticized by a public freshly introduced to the work of Karl Marx. He sought to victimize those not benefiting from the Victorian Era fashions of the day. Many couldn't participate in the rich and famous lavish lifestyles; it was easy to create a voter base and unionized members out of the victimized laborer. And to maintain that control over the public, the terms "stay in your lane" were invented to prevent upward mobility within organizations so that perpetual victimization could be maintained culturally.

The villains, of course, were those seeking to rob off that culture at every turn, and as it turned out, there was a lot of profit for the very bad in keeping people victimized and believing that heroes would never come to save them. That is always the goal of villainy, to eliminate hope and to force everyone into limited choices. That is why a gunfighter seeking to bring justice to culture would not start with the barriers to the objective, the lowlifes and pecking order peasants of that culture who stand in the way. The gunfighter would always seek the top people of that culture and deal with only those closest to them to achieve the needed objectives.

That means that you as a gunfighter don't waste time with trivial nonsense that is often going on with people of lower status, those happy to reside in the powerful gutters and roll like dogs on the floor for the table scraps of the elite. The gunfighter always looks to the locked doors and finds a way to get inside where the real deal makers are and stay close to those positions because when it comes time to pull the trigger, the target is clear and insightful. In the modern sense, the water cooler conversations about some sports event are no different than talking about the town's favorite whore in a saloon where everyone has taken their turn. Wasting time on such dialogue will not give a gunfighter a good reputation or an opportunity for advancement. Only by staying close to those most powerful and with the most intimate knowledge of how things move and shake can a gunfighter do their job. Wasting time on people wasting away is not the way to go.

It might sound cruel, but few people chose to be that way. A gunfighter does not strive to belittle people, they are constantly striving to be at the top of the food chain, and nobody will ever get there by being friendly with the lowlifes. In a saloon, lowlifes are those who have low ambitions for life; they do a little work, spend that money on drinks and entertainment, lose it all, chew some tobacco, spit it in the spittoon, then go back to work to do it all again then wonder why as older people, they have nothing and have wasted their life. What good is it to get to know anything about them, their brothers and sisters, what music they like, or anything for that matter? The answer is nothing; they aren't worth knowing. That is unless they see some way to get behind the locked doors. Otherwise, wasting time with them is a foolish enterprise. There are many in every company looking to just get along with their peers and stay in their lane. They'll say that thinking about other things is above their pay grade and not their job. Those are the losers of life. They should be avoided like a sickness because that is the state of their existence.

Focus instead as a gunfighter should only be on the top prizes in everything that is done. The bullets might not always hit their targets, but you should shoot anyway and let what may come. Get to know the top people in your company and associate with them. They are the ones worth knowing and speaking with; they know where the keys to the locked rooms are and what goes on there. When resources are limited, as they always are, wasting time on losers won't lead to wins. This goes against many modern thoughts on the matter. Know that our minds were shaped by the antics of the Victorian Era and the global forces at work and entered our culture with significant influence. But they have turned out to be wrong. If you have a chance to pick your time between two people, the spittoon spitting loser or the CEO, the answer is obvious. Nobody is perfect between the two; one is at least trying to be. And that is where the results for opportunity always are.

CHAPTER NOTES:

a. The term "stay in your lane" is an invitation to pass up the perpetrator at top speed. Don't waste time on losers; go only to the top people when possible.
b. If you follow the house rules, the villains will always prosper. Don't waste time on losers spitting in the spittoons.
c. Karl Marx sought to victimize the lazy and unambitious so that the value of the masses could limit the gains toward profit. To function within those rules is the sure way to fail.
d. The gunfighter always looks beyond the locked doors to discover for themselves where the key needs reside. Don't ever stay in your lane! Pass those who try to block you, always.

DON'T CREATE AN OUTLAW JESSE JAMES

Throughout a career, the business owner, manager, or even the up-and-coming employee climbing their way through tenacity and hope toward opportunities for a better way of life will have to deal with precisely the condition that made Jesse James. Many think of the outlaw gunman as a villain, but that depends on which side of the Civil War one fought for, and in modern culture and business life, it depends on which side of the controlling management you might happen to be on. James and his brother Frank fought in the Civil War for the South as bushwhackers, guerrilla war soldiers fighting for a cause that may have been wrong in hindsight, but they believed in it based on their times. And so it was after the war, and the Confederates had lost many in the Missouri counties around where Jesse James lived, felt suddenly displaced by the political turmoil of Union radicals taking over all their elected offices from mayors to judges in the wake of the war. The mistake was that the victors of the war representing the North felt entitled to crush what remained of the South and treated Missouri as a territory of conquest. With the war concluded, the conquered people had no recourse, and in such times there is always a challenge to the established authority, a homage to the way things were, and that's where Jesse James came to be. Instead of accepting this new regime, Jesse formed a gang of traditionalists with his brother and challenged this new authority. He became a hero to the South and a menace to the North.

Over many years of business operation, these kinds of transfers of power happen constantly. Management friendly to your position is bound to happen, and of course, the situation will switch at some point, and a new band of authority figures will take over management for whatever reason. It happens politically as well among our countries, and always the new power base seeks to put its foot down on the necks of their new subserviates. It would be nice to say that such occasions only occur sometimes, but the truth is that it is consistent with the assumption of "always." That means that being a successful business manager or owner means constantly navigating this trend to keep your organization viable, even as internal strife threatens to derail everything all the time. A million Jesse James types are working at all levels of society at any given point worldwide. Jesse James was remembered mainly because the media chronicled his antics as passive-aggressive supporters of pre-Civil War life and was looking for someone to represent their anger to the world. For them, Frank and Jesse James represented freedom from this new tyranny, or at least a chance to resume the success of their previous lives.

As it turns out, Jesse James and his brother were frequent friends of very good lawmen such as Bat Masterson, Wyatt Earp, and many other law and order types who were taming areas like Dodge City. Frank James would end up in Buffalo Bill's Wild West Show years after the end of Jesse James' acts of rebellion. When we talk about the James Brothers, we're not talking about radical outlaws who were bloodthirsty villains, but people who, correct or not, felt they had to defend their way of life from an encroaching foreign culture. Different cultures defined law and order in this case. That is how things are in all cultures; everyone believes their culture is the best, their way of life the most promising; however, the truth can only be determined by a fight of some kind where the better idea or culture emerges victorious. Without that victory, there will always be discontent among the people.

When there is a change at the board of director positions or upper management, care must always be made not to give rise to another Jesse James within your culture. But in some cases, the reader may be that Jesse James and a challenge to an oppressive system of controls may be needed. As it turned out, there was much tolerance for the violence of Jesse James, even to the present day. That is until the radical Union political emplacements wore out and Southern sympathizers began to return to elected offices. Once this occurred, the people of Missouri found themselves not wanting the bloodshed of the James Brothers and their bank robberies and swashbuckling attacks on the remnants of the war-torn years. People will always support outlaws and terrorists to rage against a machine because they lack the courage to do it themselves. That is the same in any form of business management in the modern corporate setting. But once people feel they again have a voice in the system, they lose patience quickly for rebellion and return to seeking peace in their day-to-day lives. In the case of Jesse James, that is when the world turned on him, and he was more valuable dead than alive. Even at the height of his bounty, people all over the South would shelter the James gang eagerly. It was their way of poking their suppressors in the eye. Yet once that wore off and the suppressors grew tired of their tyranny, then those former friends of Jesse James started plotting his death, which didn't take long.

This little lesson is very applicable to this very day. In the climbs for power within an organization, keep in mind these basic rules. If you are the suppressor, avoid making a Jesse James in your culture to attack everything you are trying to build in the bathrooms, boardrooms, and executive suites. If you are the Jesse James type, know that your window for rebellion lasts only as long as the boots rest on the necks of those under the new regime with a heavy heave. Once the audaciousness rubs off and drifts away back into complacency, tolerance for radicalism will diminish quickly. Often the actions of a Jesse James are needed when an unjust world is upon us, but the window does not stay open long. Victory is not always so easy to see, and all the sums of bold actions don't always measure out directly in more gold for your pockets, but rather in a less oppressive culture to operate in. Justice is not always easy to see. But Jesse James never noticed when it was time to put away the ways of bushwhacking and go back to being a productive contributor to his society. Once the smell of gun smoke takes over such a personality, it is hard to re-holster the means to peace and prosperity. But any good gunfighter must learn this lesson eventually, or they will end up the way Jesse James did. They may be eradicated from the earth and remembered as legends. But they won't be around well enough to enjoy their spoils of war, and in the world of business, that is not how you play the game. You play to win and to enjoy the spoils of victory. Not to simply be placed in a shallow grave on the family farm.

CHAPTER NOTES:

a. When a culture change is introduced and management changes hands, be careful not to impose too much on the conquered culture that they might feel is disgraceful, such as what happened with Jesse James after the Civil War.
b. An established authority needs to unify their culture, not to separate it with heavy-handed imposition. Humans, because of their need to rebel, will undermine your culture if you do.
c. There are millions of Jesse James types working at every level of society. Incorporate them in your culture, don't let them terrorize the good from the shadows.
d. If you are the Jesse James type, it is your nature to do what you do, and if the management is unjust, they deserve to be challenged in any way possible.

MANAGING PRESSURE IS THE KEY TO SUCCESS

This book started in the mountains of Japan, specifically Himeji Castle and the temples in the surrounding area. I was fortunate enough to have a lovely lunch at a samurai encampment dedicated to the castle back in those feudal days of Japan's history. Around that time, I started Cowboy Fast Draw and was learning the sport to manage stress professionally. The combination of those events ignited some evolutionary thoughts, especially in the many Lean manufacturing events that are now very common in western business practices. And now the book has ended on the windswept plains just a few miles outside of Roswell, New Mexico, in weather 0 degrees with snow-packed up around my RV. It was a long quest to dust off a large gold nugget that many considered was just a clump of clay that came to light and brought forth the miracles of Western Civilization and the business practices that brought wealth to the world for all who dare reach for it. I walked in the footsteps of Billy the Kid and Pat Garrett in New Mexico and thought hard about the Lincoln County War between two business factions and contemplated the morality of the great John Chisum who had his big ranch just outside of Roswell. There were other places, but sometimes you can't understand something fully until you've walked in the footsteps, and I can say that I have. There were other countries too, but looking out the window on a blistering cold day in New Mexico into downtown Roswell, it all became apparent. There Natural Law arrived on the backs of John Chisum to combat the evil of misdirected souls; the key to all management in Western Civilization outlined in this book came to light by essentially managing pressure.

The greatest thing I have learned in Cowboy Fast Draw was in reloading my ammunition. For that sport, it's not too complicated. It requires a shell casing, a 209-shotgun primer just set into the recess of the shell, and a wax bullet placed into the other end. Gunpowder is not needed; the pressure which fires the wax bullet comes directly from the primer. It was effortless to load, so of course, this started me into getting actual presses and formally reloading lead bullets with gunpowder and seating everything correctly with different combinations to manipulate the way a bullet behaves when fired. And it is within this process that the summation of this book's conclusions rest. Shooting a gun is not about the gun; the gun is only a tool. It helps you direct the science of a bullet going off toward a target. What makes a gun and a gunfighter specifically effective is how they manage that pressure created by the explosion of a bullet. It's not the gun itself. For instance, Billy the Kid had a method of holding his hand with his index finger pointed toward the target to shoot straight under duress, but it was the bullet that did all the work. Wild Bill was exceptionally calm under fire when he faced down a challenger in a duel, but it was still the management of the bullet firing that did most of the work. It was sheer audacity that Jesse James utilized to mow down his foes, but it was the management of firing a bullet that was the actual sender of much lead payment. In that way, the gunfighter is the manager of the lead currency, which comes from the explosive contents within a gun's chambers. So, in that way, the modern manager in common ways up and coming, or at the top of the pecking order in a vast economy of many dangerous turns, the similarity between gunfighter and modern business manager find themselves related.

Many other business methods of Leaning out a process or convincing people to do things you need them to do involve consensus-building and building teams of shared responsibility. It sounds great from the perspective of a dandy riding in on a train into a town already tamed by the great gunfighters, but such methods never work when left on their own in a business culture still wild and wooly from its inception. Therefore, managing pressure is the key to managing anything and everything. By Natural Law, there are always destructive forces at play in every activity touched by the eyes of humanity. The gunpowder exists in nature, the metal of a good gun exists in nature, the practice of putting these forces together as a tool to capture natural violence and to direct it toward a helpful end is unique and special. It is the key to a successful life in Western Civilization and all the business conducted under such an umbrella. It serves as an example to the world of how they could improve their lives if only they dared to follow. But first, it must be understood that the bullet has all the keys to that future, directing the pressure from bullets and using the gun to control them. Or in the modern sense, in how the sound manager and business owner direct that pressure toward a goal well defined and left to the obscurity of collective determination, which often can never agree on anything. Therefore, the essence of leadership is in understanding and managing pressure, just as the gunfighters of America did to bring Natural Law to the vast reaches of an ambitious civilization propelling itself westward toward an undefined destiny, all in the pursuit of personal freedom. That is how John Chisum came to own and operate a large ranch outside of Roswell and involved much of what we now call New Mexico. He did it out of a need to be free and prosperous, and the result was an industry that brought life where it hadn't been developed before.

In all places such as Lincoln County, New Mexico, Dodge City, Kansas City, Missouri, and Deadwood, South Dakota, gunfighters and businesspeople—sometimes both—did what Indians never could. Because the key was not yielding to pressure as humans had been doing for thousands of years—But managing the pressures that were always there and putting them to good use. That settled a matter I had been thinking about for over 30 professional years and why the Lean seminars never seemed to get the point. In my visit to the samurai garden for that nice lunch I mentioned, the pressure behind management was the answer and was found in the West to the questions that were on everyone's minds. Everyone involved is always brilliant, but there seems to be always something missing in understanding the true essence of business exchange. In the samurai culture, the work with the samurai sword worked a melee weapon to effectiveness, like a bow, for instance, or a spear. It was a noble form of combat, but it lacked the speed that the modern era demanded. The Western Civilization development of the gun, precisely the innovations made by Sam Colt and the Henry Repeaters, the capacity for effectiveness was in managing a lot more pressure within the case of a bullet. This was a lot faster form of combat that advanced American society to the top of the food chain in economics worldwide. Thinking like a gunfighter is an excellent thing to do with the modern businessperson and is the key to much health and true happiness—and of course, the profits that drive the world.

CHAPTER NOTES:

a. By studying the nature of a bullet, it becomes clear that a gun is not the critical thing to consider; it's in the explosion that takes place in a bullet.
b. It is up to the gun to point that pressure in the correct direction by creating an explosion, where justice is needed. The gunfighter ensures that the gun is managed correctly.
c. Putting the focus on a gun and not the bullet, most will miss the point. It's not in the shooting of the gun that matters; it's about creating the pressure within the gun and pointing that pressure where it needs to go.
d. Creating pressure in business is the key to everything that occurs toward the aims of profit and success. Managing that pressure will decide who wins and who loses and how the future is determined.

ABOUT THE AUTHOR

Rich Hoffman is a political consultant and business advisor in the Cincinnati area. As a Lean Manufacturing practitioner for over 30 years, he has combined his experiences with the Cowboy Fast Draw Association to present this revealing perspective on western business conduct and its great value to the world. Additionally, he has been a talk radio host and written two previous books on political philosophy, The Symposium of Justice and Tail of the Dragon. As an award-winning Wild West performer over several decades, this new analysis of strategy in business will bring shooting from the hip into a new perspective. Hoffman supports various firearms organizations proudly, such as The Ohio Fast Draw Association, the NRA, and Second Call Defense. You can learn more at gunfighterguide.shop.

CPSIA information can be obtained
at www.ICGtesting.com
Printed in the USA
LVHW031558220821
695841LV00001B/134

9 781662 823206